Japanese Minimalism:
Your Personal Guide to The Art Of Minimalist Living

Nicole Garrod

ISBN: 9798692556783
Cover and graphical design: www.latoadv.it

© Copyright 2020 - All rights reserved.

The content contained within this book may not be reproduced, duplicated or transmitted without direct written permission from the author or the publisher.

Under no circumstances will any blame or legal responsibility be held against the publisher, or author, for any damages, reparation, or monetary loss due to the information contained within this book, either directly or indirectly.

Legal Notice:

This book is copyright protected. It is only for personal use. You cannot amend, distribute, sell, use, quote or paraphrase any part, or the content within this book, without the consent of the author or publisher.

Disclaimer Notice:

Please note the information contained within this document is for educational and entertainment purposes only. All effort has been executed to present accurate, up to date, reliable, complete information. No warranties of any kind are declared or implied. Readers acknowledge that the author is not engaged in the rendering of legal, financial, medical or professional advice. The content within this book has been derived from various sources. Please consult a licensed professional before attempting any techniques outlined in this book.

By reading this document, the reader agrees that under no circumstances is the author responsible for any losses, direct or indirect, that are incurred as a result of the use of the information contained within this document, including, but not limited to, errors, omissions, or inaccuracies.

CONTENTS

INTRODUCTION 1
THE PITFALLS OF CONSUMERISM 6
THE BENEFITS OF MINIMALISM 14
WHY JAPANESE MINIMALISM IS THE BEST 22
    The Differences Between Western and Japanese Minimalism 22
    How Japanese Minimalism Can Help You Live A Better Life 30
WABI-SABI AND JAPANESE MINIMALISM 33
    The Beauty of Wabi-Sabi 35
    The Unique Bond Between Wabi-Sabi and Japanese Minimalism 40
    The 7 Principles to Help You Adopt Wabi-Sabi and Japanese Minimalism 42

        #1: Kanso 42

        #2: Fukinsei 45

        #3, #4, #5: Shibumi, Shizen and Yugen 47

        #6 & #7: Datsuzoku and Seijaku 49

THE MOST EFFECTIVE KONMARI DECLUTTERING TECHNIQUE: TIPS & HACKS 51
    The KonMari method and Japanese Minimalism: The Link 51
    Basic Guidelines to Help You Master the KonMari Method 52
    The Ultimate Category-by-Category Decluttering Plan 58
HOW TO APPLY JAPANESE MINIMALIS TO YOUR WORK AND PROFESSIONAL LIFE 65
    Minimalism and Your Work Life 65
    Steps to Help You Apply Minimalism to Your Professional Life 69
HOW TO CREATE A JAPANESE MINIMALISM INSPIRED LIFESTILE 82
    Minimalism and Food 82
    Minimalism and Sleep 86
    Minimalism and Fitness 88

Minimalism and Relationships 90
Minimalism and Finances 91
Minimalism and Spirituality 92
CONCLUSIONS 94
BIBLIOGRAPHY 95

INTRODUCTION

Modern life has become a rat race, and wherever you look, you'll see people competing to gain more wealth, success, money, material possessions, power, etc.

What many people fail to understand is that this contest to have more and be more is more harmful than it is beneficial. It causes us to pursue endeavors that seem good and meaningful on the surface, but, upon further interrogation, reveal themselves as worthless.

For example, consider this:

- *We work round the clock to buy a bigger house. Upon doing so and shortly after the newness of it all wears off, we realize that we have to work even harder to furnish it with luxurious household items to match, which throws us into the realm of discontented unhappiness.*

- *We push ourselves hard, burn the midnight oil, and compromise our values to please "an ungrateful boss who can fire us at a moment's notice".*

- *We sacrifice time with loved ones to meet deadlines.*

- *We never really rest because we have a never-ending pile of tasks, many of which don't truly align with our deepest desire.*

- *We also pursue particular career paths not because it's what we want, but because from a very young age, society drums into us the notion that working hard in "certain careers" is the only way to "make more money and afford the luxuries of life".*

Unfortunately, somehow, for many of us, *"earning more money and living a luxurious life"* has become our primary driver, not because that's what we truly want, but because we've bought into dogmatic societal expectations.

A sorrier fact is that after doing that all our lives, many of us reach our deathbeds unfulfilled, with nothing but a heart full of regrets.

When on your deathbed, what regrets will you have?

Bronnie Ware is an Australian nurse who has spent a good chunk of her life caring for different hospice patients in their last few weeks of life.

From her work, she recorded all their dying wishes in a blog titled Inspiration and Chai, that she turned later into a bestselling book titled *The Top Five Regrets of the Dying*.

In the book, she talks about the impressive clarity the dying has in the last days of their lives and how that clarity can help us make wiser life decisions. Ware mentions how similar themes repeatedly surfaced when the patients talked about their regrets and wishes in life.

At the top of her list of the five primary regrets of the dying was this regret — *not per verbatim:*

> *"I wish I'd dared to live a life true to myself instead of a life dictated by what others expected of me".*

If you analyze this regret a bit more deeply, you will realize that two primary reasons are the cause of our failure to live a genuine life. Those are:

1. First, many of us are not self-aware, because of which we are never sure about what we genuinely want or who we are within.

2. Secondly, where we know who we are and what we genuinely want, many of us lack the courage to pursue it mainly because we cannot break free from the shackles of a stereotypical society.

Another regret expressed by many of the hospice patients under Bronnie Ware's care was—*per verbatim this time:*

JAPANESE MINIMALISM

> *"I wish I hadn't worked so hard".*

Why this regret is so common among the dying is easy to see. Because after "working so hard", many of them had missed beautiful moments with spouses, kids, friends, and loved ones, all because they were "breadwinners who felt they had to work hard to earn a living".

Following this regret was another common regret—*per verbatim also:*

> *"I wish I had let myself be happier".*

If you delve deeper into these regrets, you will realize that the need to work hard stems from wanting to be more and achieve more, both of which thrive on the notion that *having more is better and a sign of success*, which is not always the case because more is not always better.

Many of us mistakenly equate having more money, material gains, more victories, more possessions, a bigger house, a bigger car, and everything expensive to happiness or contentment in life.

Because of buying into this false belief, when given a choice between pursuing our heart's desires but never earning a penny from it and doing something we hate but that can make us a lot of money, many of us would jump at the latter option, which is rather sad.

These three of the five primary regrets of the dying detailed by Bronnie Ware reveal why many of us fail to live the lives of our dreams. We've allowed societal doctrines, media biases, consumerism, and shiny object syndrome to blind us to the truth, which is that:

- *If it's not what your heart genuinely wants, it makes no sense to have a big house decorated with gorgeous crystal chandeliers, elegant leather sofas, the best delicacies money can buy, but no memories to cherish.*

- *Being at the top of your career, with great accolades to your name, but no health and mental peace to enjoy your accomplishments because you've worked yourself into a deathbed is worthless.*

Although we often feel that we need a lot to be happy, peaceful, and prosperous, the reality is much simpler, and the wise words of Vernon Howard, a spiritual teacher, bestselling author, and philosopher, can sum it up:

> *"You have succeeded in life when all you really want is only what you really need".*

To be happy and successful in life, you don't need a lot. With a few basic needs and loved ones to celebrate your daily life with, you can live a happy life.

Unfortunately, most of us come to this realization when it is too late, often after we've spent our youth, time, energy, and money pursuing "shiny objects" that are far from our hearts' genuine desire.

Do you:

- *Want to get to your deathbed with a smile on your face instead of regrets in your heart?*

- *Wish to pursue the things that stir your heart, not what your parents, family, or society expect of—or want—for you?*

- *Desire to live a simple life governed and driven by your genuine aspirations instead of superficial wishes, consumerism, and societal indoctrination?*

If so, embracing the principles of ***Japanese Minimalism*** and making them part of your daily life can help you live a simple, happy life where every day, you wake up smiling, eager for the day because you are living your dream life.

Read on to discover why Japanese minimalism could be the secret to your best life yet!

Japanese minimalism is the Japanese version of minimalism. It differs from Western minimalism in the sense that it focuses more on helping you distill clarity, peacefulness, and happiness into your life.

Japanese minimalism is what you should embrace if you wish to live a meaningful, empowered, and prosperous life where you know what you want and are not afraid to pursue it.

This book will reveal everything you need to know about Japanese minimalism, including:

- *The pitfalls of consumerism*

- *The benefits you stand to derive from incorporating Japanese minimalism into your life*

- *How to use Japanese minimalism principles to make a slow, gradual, and successful transition to a more fulfilling, well-rounded, and thriving life*

- *Why pursuing shiny objects and meaningless temptations and desires will lead to deathbed regrets, and how Japanese minimalism can help you avoid that dreadful end.*

- **And so much, much more.**

After reading this book, you will have the motivation to make some remarkable and meaningful changes in your life and will know the steps you need to take to start living the life of your dreams.

I would like to express you my gratitude for choosing this book, I really hope that can help you to begin your self-discovery journey and manifesting your heart's desire and reality. Make sure to leave a short review on Amazon, I'd really love to hear about your thoughts.

1.

THE PITFALLS OF CONSUMERISM

In the last several decades, we've seen rampant development and the rise of consumerism.

At first glance, both seem like good things. However, upon further interrogation, they prove downright problematic because we are now consuming our resources at an alarming pace that exceeds the rate at which our planet can replenish those resources.

Estimates predict that if all of the earth's populace consumed the same quantity of resources U.S. citizens do on average, we would need around 4 Earth-like planets to sustain human life. When you factor in other wealthier, "first-world" countries, estimates show that we would need 5.4 Earth-like planets to support the human species.

Besides compromising sustainability, consumerism and rampant development have detrimentally changed our beliefs and thoughts. Today, we focus more on quantity and less on quality, which has disrupted our quality of life and kept us from pursuing our genuine needs.

Because playing into the hands of consumerism and development is one of the primary causes of unfulfilled lives, let's discuss the pitfalls of consumerism.

Global inequality

The ever-rising rate of resource consumption in wealthier nations has widened the gap between the poor and the rich, giving credence to the old age adage, *"the rich get richer, while the poor become poorer".*

In 2005, 10% of the wealthiest population worldwide consumed around 59% of the resources on the globe. The poorest 10% of the lot accounted for a mere 0.5% of the total global resource utilization.

If we observe economic spending trends and how to utilize our money better, estimates show that we would need 6 billion U.S. dollars to provide primary education to kids worldwide and 22 billion U.S. dollars to give every human access to hygienic drinking water, nutrition, and health services.

Sadly, our actual spending is nowhere near close to being that meaningful: Every year, Europeans spend approximately 11 billion U.S. dollars on ice cream alone, which is two times what we would need to educate every child on this planet every year.

Moreover, alone, Europe spends more than 50 billion U.S. dollars on cigarettes, while, globally, we spend as much as 400 billion U.S. dollars on narcotics. These statistics paint a bleak picture that continues turning grimmer over time, especially as we become more and more *"developed and globalized"*.

Can you imagine how much we could accomplish as a species if we could reduce our consumption by a mere fraction?

For instance, reducing our consumption by a mere 10% and then directing the monies freed-up to worthwhile causes could drastically and remarkably improve the lives of the underprivileged people across the globe.

Increased obesity rate

There's a close correlation between consumerism and the increase, alarming cases of obesity across the globe. That should not surprise you; after all, consumerism focuses on using as much as possible instead of using what we need.

Overconsumption has a domino effect on many societal issues. For instance, consumption raises obesity cases, which causes other social and cultural problems like stretched-thin medical services and a lower human resource capacity. In the US., the per capita medical expenses of those suffering from obesity are about $2,500 higher than average.

Higher pollution

Consumerism also causes a lot of environmental issues. Consider this: as demand for certain goods rises, manufacturers have to use more resources to produce those goods, which leads to increased use of land, more deforestation, and higher pollutant emissions that worsen climate change.

The planet is currently experiencing a devastating decrease in water supplies because intense farming procedures are over-taxing our water resources.

Proper and safe water disposal is another problem; today, many have resorted to using our oceans as a major dumpsite.

More than 50% of the plastic manufactured every year is single use only. Once used, it makes its way to an ocean or a landfill. Scientists have stated that around 12 million tons of plastic flood the sea annually, creating massive floating islands of garbage.

Consumerism keeps you from knowing what you want.

One of the biggest pitfalls of consumerism and rampant development is that the two keep you from clarifying what you want to do with your life.

Think of it this way: Naturally, when you are busy working 8 hours a day at a full-time job, a few more hours to your side hustle, and more time to showering, cleaning, cooking, and completing routine chores, you don't have much time left to be with yourself.

Not having some "me time": makes determining what you truly need difficult. This problem becomes apparent when you realize how little time, we have left to live our lives and do the things that genuinely matter to us. When we don't have time for ourselves, we fail to dig deeper into who we are and what we want in life.

Perhaps you've always wanted to fulfill your life-long dream of being an author of children's books, and you feel you could be happy doing that. Unfortunately, thanks to consumerism and your desire to buy more and be more, you feel compelled to pursue a six-figure job that doesn't make you happy.

Amidst all the running around day in and day out, and letting worthless fancies guide you, you never have time to dig deep into what you want, or to pause and enjoy the moments of life that matter. In the end, even though you have money, you end up feeling disconnected from your life.

Similarly, your genuine desire could be contentment in life. However, because you are not in tune with this desire, you end up seeking joy in an expensive Rolex, a Gucci handbag, or a Mercedes.

The pursuit of these worldly possessions keeps you too busy to have time to celebrate your son's victory in a school competition. It keeps you from savoring a few more minutes in bed with your spouse or spending time with friends, which may be what you want, but because you're too busy "making money", you never have enough time for it.

When you stop chasing worldly gains and dig deeper into what you genuinely want, it becomes easier to realize your genuine needs, which are probably not owning a Rolex or the best-looking car on the block.

Heightened levels of stress, anxiety, and depression

It's okay to obsess over work now and then. However, if workaholism takes over your life and you work from the moment you wake up to the moment you get back to bed late at night, your only results will be psychological and chronic health issues.

Today, psychological conditions like stress, anxiety, depression, eating disorders, and personality disorders are a pressing concern. The stats are only rising as time passes, and, as unbelievable as it sounds, we can correlate these conditions with consumerism, media biases, and meaningless desires.

Let's use an example to illustrate this: Because they know that many people—especially women—are "discontented" with how they look, modern media adverts incline towards showing how happiness comes from having a size zero figure, bigger butt, or fairer skin.

Because these adverts are so convincing—advertisers are notoriously good at using psychological manipulation—many women end up buying and hoarding every fairness creams on the market, saving for years to get butt implants, etc.

Unfortunately, because those desires do not come from a healthy place, even after buying every fairness cream on the market, saving for months or years to get Lip or butt augmentation, many people end up dissatisfied.

Here's another example: When the media portrays owning luxury furniture as the ultimate path to inner peace and happiness, many of us eagerly spend thousands of dollars on that.

Later on, it dawns on us that costly material possessions don't add happiness to our lives; they add worry and apprehension. We also realize that we would have been much better off utilizing the same amount of money on something more meaningful. This realization leads to self-disappointment and sadness

Education is another typical example: Many of us think that studying in top-tier, expensive colleges is the only way to get the best education and live a meaningful, happy life; that is not the case. Other, less costly colleges can give you the same knowledge you would get at Harvey Mudd.

The primary difference between institutions of higher learning is the educational experience, which means you don't need to get into generational debt to get a good education. Chronic stress, anxiety, and depression are a result of feeling disconnected from your life, troubled from within, and unaccomplished.

When you cannot live life on your terms, have no loved ones with whom to celebrate little moments of joy, and no time freedom to pursue your heart's desires, you will live a stressed and depressed existence, which is no way to live life.

Increased consumer debt

According to a report by the U.S. Department of Commerce, from 1982 onwards, the personal savings rate of U.S. citizens has dropped to zero from 11%.

Additionally, personal bankruptcy filings and debt have continued to increase each year. Findings from the Federal Reserve Board show that the amount stood at around $554 billion in 1997 but grew to a whopping $730 billion in 2002.

Moreover, a survey conducted in 1998 by student loan provider Nellie Mae showed that about 80% of undergraduate students owned a minimum of one credit card.

We can relate the ever-growing rise of consumer debt to consumerism—the name, *consumer debt*, says it all.

Modern consumers are victims of advertisements centered on media biases that compel them to have the best of everything as the way to a happy and meaningful life, even when such costly purchases lead to life-long debt.

Can you relate to this? Have you made a costly, debt-funded purchase driven by a desire to own the latest trendy fashion item? Perhaps you wanted to purchase the latest iPhone, but because you didn't have enough money, had to accrue $500 in costly credit card debt?

Perhaps you can relate to taking on a mortgage that puts a roof over your head, yes, but that also keeps you from backpacking through Asia, which is what you have always wanted to do.

Whatever the case, remember that any debt you pile on does more than create financial burdens; it also adds to your routine financial duress and tension. Think about it:

How is a loan of $20,000 for a vacation to Bora Bora benefitting you when all it does is raise your stress and anxiety and deprive you of the financial security you could enjoy by making wiser financial decisions?

Increased hoarding and materialistic attachment

Hoarding, which is more than living in a cluttered space, is a major, 21st-century concern.

You struggle with 'hoarding disorder' when you keep things that don't add value to your life or that interfere with your legal, financial, emotional, social, and physical wellbeing.

According to Catherine Ayers, a renowned geriatric psychologist who works at the University of California and has created a CBT (cognitive behavior therapy) program for those struggling with hoarding disorder, if you have a refrigerator full of expired goods, you suffer from the hoarding disorder. If you have a disorganized nature that keeps you from maintaining a health care routine or your appointments, you also suffer from the hoarding disorder.

Studies on the subject reveal that around 6% of Americans, which is about 19 million people, struggle with compulsive hoarding.

Earlier in the century, hoarding fell under the category of Obsessive-Compulsive Disorders (OCD). In recent years, however, its rate has increased so much that now, it has a separate categorical classification.

Brain imaging studies conducted on hoarders show very low activity in their anterior cingulate cortex, a region of the brain involved in active thinking and emotional regulation. When hoarders see different trigger images, including pictures of people discarding or shredding things, it hyper-activates that region of the brain.

A primary cause of hoarding and the hoarding disorder is the undue and extravagant meaning we attach to material possessions.

For instance, when you think you will need empty cartons and boxes later, you may give in to the temptation to hoard them to the point of dedicating rooms to them.

When you feel sure you will use your prom dress later in life, you will feel compelled to save it and other dresses you have outgrown for years.

When you feel attached to your notebooks, drawings, and journals from high school, you cannot bring yourself to part with them because they take you down memory lane.

When you see a pack of 3 ketchup bottles on discount at the grocery store, you may purchase the valuable seeming offer even though you don't use ketchup.

That is how we attach meanings such as 'joy,' 'value,' 'comfort,' 'care,' 'nostalgia,' 'love,' 'warmth,' 'luxury,' 'class,' 'elegance' and other labels to material possessions.

A pearl necklace turns into an object of class and luxury that helps you stand out; dozens of comic books turn into memorabilia of your past. No matter which reasons you have for hoarding, the bottom line this:

Hoarding is not healthy and beneficial; it only makes you a victim of consumerism.

We quest for more and bigger stuff

The need to have more things leads to a quest for bigger spaces and remote storage spaces.

When your two-bedroom apartment does not have sufficient space to accommodate your boxes of gadgets, utensils, books, magazines, old clothes, nuts, bolts, and the likes, you feel compelled to rent storage spaces to house your belongings. While doing so may seem practical, adopting such an approach is illogical because if you haven't used something, the chances are high that you will never use it.

Because it's primarily about living a simple life full of value and meaning, minimalism can limit the effects of these issues, and as you will see in the next chapter, it has tons of other benefits.

2.

THE BENEFITS OF MINIMALISM

Many of us use minimalism and frugal living interchangeably, but the two are different concepts altogether.

Frugal living is more about spending less and opting for cheaper alternatives to luxurious or expensive products.

On its part, minimalism is a way of life/lifestyle that operates on the principles of filling your life with things that bring you joy and meaning. Minimalism is more about creating a meaningful life guided by your real needs instead of superficial wants.

Many people mistake 'minimalism' for having less or opting for economical options; the truth couldn't be further.

The Western or American version of minimalism believes in understanding and acknowledging your genuine needs, which, coincidentally, aren't that many, and then sticking to things, values, people, and activities that help fulfill those needs.

With minimalism, you don't have to give up your car. If it adds value to your life in any way, you can keep it. On the other hand, if you have other things that don't add value to your life, say, a T.V. you never watch, the ten pairs of sneakers you never wear, and dozens of DVDs you haven't touched in ages, you should get rid of those.

When you let go of the unnecessary things in your life, you create room for clarity and peace of mind to focus on everything you truly want to think about and pursue because it adds value to your existence.

Besides that, here is how minimalism helps you live a meaningful and empowered life.

It creates physical and mental space

When you have gazillion things to maintain and care for, you will feel mentally and physically exhausted.

The furniture pieces, utensils, dishes, and cars you have to clean, and the countless other things lying all over your house waiting for you to tend to them use up a lot of energy.

Cleaning and maintaining things are physically exhausting and mentally taxing, more so when you have to worry about your possessions. This situation changes for the better when you let go of what's unnecessary in your life. When you adopt a minimalistic approach to life, you start to keep what you need, which reduces your effort, work, and exhaustion.

For example, when your lounge has a few chairs instead of 10, naturally, your cleaning needs will be lower. Moreover, when you know you won't see a pile of tangled cables and wires when you open your desk's drawer, you feel mentally at peace.

Entering a house full of physical clutter leads to mental chaos and exhaustion. Once you get rid of that, you create mental space, peacefulness, and relaxation.

It helps you keep what's essential

Minimalism is more than about decluttering and organizing your house and workspace. It is also about letting go of meaningless activities, ideas, and people.

When you embrace minimalism, you assess the value of your social contacts, relationships, activities, and your beliefs you nurture. Then, you gradually let go of everything that feels toxic or limits your emotional, spiritual, professional, and personal growth.

The act of freeing yourself from unimportant things, people, engagements, and beliefs brings you peace, joy, value, and comfort. It helps you surround yourself with valuable things, meaning, happiness, and avoid all kinds of negativity.

It saves time, effort, and energy

Naturally, when you have less stuff to clean, maintain, and worry about, you save the extra time, effort, and energy you would have otherwise used to clean and organize these things.

Think of how relaxed you would feel when you don't have to clean dozens of dishes thrice a day or organize heaps of clothes in your wardrobe every day. That can only happen when you incorporate minimalism into your life.

Once you embrace minimalism, you won't waste hours and ounces of energy in worrying about things. Because you won't have myriads of things to worry about, you will keep everything in an orderly fashion.

It makes it easier to find things

If your wardrobe is a dumping ground for all your clothes, where coats intertwine with shirts and pants with sweaters and socks, it will take longer to find something decent to wear. Similarly, if documents, files, and stationery clutter your workspace desk, the chaos will make it challenging to find what you need.

When you embrace minimalism and integrate it into spaces such as your home, you slowly eliminate the things you don't need, use, or want. All useless, broken, old, meaningless, and extra things make their way out of your home, because of which you start enjoying a more spacious house.

Your decluttered space becomes a haven for the things you need, and gradually, everything starts to find its rightful place or spot.

Your car keys start always being on the hook beside the entrance door. Your pens find a home in their holder, notebooks on the shelf, and clothes on their hangers.

This system adds structure to your home and life and makes it easier to find the things you need quickly.

Minimalism can help you enjoy more freedom

Accumulating things is an anchor that ties us down.

The instant we own something, especially something expensive, we become apprehensive of losing it. This fear weighs us down and triggers our anxieties.

On the contrary, when you let go of what's meaningless, you invite freedom into your life; this newfound freedom leaves you feeling free and relaxed. You feel free from debt, greed, overworking, exhaustion, stress, obsession, accumulating things, and the need to do and be more.

It gives you a chance to pursue exciting hobbies

When you don't feel the urge to stroll through Home Depot and Pottery Barn aisles hunting for a bargain for your already-full lounge, you create more time and spaces for things you love, but that you could not find the time to engage in because of "being too busy".

Although many people complain about lacking time to do things they want, many never think about what they spend their time doing.

When you don't spend all your time drinking beer with colleagues, gossiping about your boss, you will have time to read your kids' bedtime stories, something you have wanted to do for a long time. When you don't spend all your time window shopping online, you will have the time to meditate, paint, or enjoy a nice, warm bath.

Enhanced peace of mind

The many things we choose to keep around us are mere distractions that we use to fill voids in our lives. Money can buy us comfort and convenience, never happiness:

*happiness is a choice you make by
enjoying whatever you have right now.*

Advertisements that covertly promise peace, prosperity, and joy from material possessions do no such thing; they only cloud our thought process and judgment.

Because of such advertisements, we start nurturing scores of meaningless temptations that weigh us down and distract us from what's truly important in our life.

For instance, if you are trying to find your sense of purpose in life, you may forget all about it the moment you see an advert of a luxury car that catches your fancy. Clinging to materialistic possessions causes more stress because it causes a level of material attachment that leaves you scared of losing those things.

When you gradually free your life from what lacks value, you let go of unnecessary attachment and invite a stream of peacefulness and calm into your life.

Moreover, detachment gives you a level of peace of mind that gives you time to think clearly about your genuine needs and aspirations and set meaningful goals around them. Instead of chasing material gains, you pursue goals you genuinely want to achieve, which allows you to start creating a meaningful life.

It can make you more focused, confident, and empowered

As you declutter your life, you start gravitating towards what you consider valuable because you have fewer distractions to battle.

This clarity increases your level of focus, which allows you to concentrate better on significant tasks and perform better at activities, thereby yielding better results. Better focus improves your efficiency and productivity, helping you achieve growth in things that matter the most to you.

Additionally, getting rid of extra and meaningless things also frees you from the unnecessary burden of the fear of failure. When you are free from undue fear, you move forward with confidence and pride.

You become well aware of what you want and how different choices can pan out for you. This clarity and awareness allow you to make informed decisions that can help you achieve what you want.

As you start to make good decisions and living life on your terms, you feel more empowered and confident. Even when particular decisions don't pan out as planned, you learn to take accountability, which boosts your self-belief and self-confidence.

More time for yourself and loved ones

Pursuing worldly gains and possessions is stressful and unhealthy because it causes you to go after things you don't need. As you take part in this rat race, you forget to tend to yourself and your loved ones.

Since we are all looking after our wellbeing, when you don't give loved ones enough time, attention, and love, it creates distance, which leaves you feeling lonely and sad. Loneliness and dejection cause depression and similar mood disorders. Minimalism can hedge against such situations.

When you free yourself from the need to work long hours or engage in meaningless activities, you create time pockets that you can use to be by yourself or with loved ones.

As you slowly connect with loved ones or reach to mend strained bond, a splash of color returns to your life, and you start experiencing the happiness, warmth, and value that comes from having meaningful relationships.

Moreover, the more quality time you spend with yourself, the more you accept, like, and respect yourself.

For instance, spending more quality time with yourself helps you eliminate self-sabotaging behaviors such as demeaning yourself in front of others, self-comparisons, trying to copy other people, pleasing others for ulterior motives and gains, or body shaming.

When you start embracing the real you, you start feeling comfortable in your skin and with your life, which helps you begin nurturing contentment and gratitude, both of which are powerful qualities that can improve your quality of life.

Financial Freedom

Contrary to popular belief, financial freedom is more than about earning more money. Financial freedom is about having enough to support your needs without accruing debt, a state that is relatively easy to achieve when you reduce unnecessary expenditures and only spend money on what you need, which is often very basic.

As you gradually overcome consumerism and stop falling prey to media biases, you slowly learn to manage your finance-related temptations better. Instead of giving in to your urges to make impulsive, costly, and meaningless purchases, you focus on saving money for the things you want because they matter. This change helps you grow your funds and have savings that you can use to pursue better things.

As you can see, minimalism can add and sustain peace, clarity, value, and meaning into your life.

Minimalism is a beautiful way of life that can help you gain freedom and liberation from unhealthy behaviors and practices that decrease your chances of happiness and inner peace.

Worth noting and mentioning here is that there are differences between American and Japanese minimalism.

Western minimalism, especially the kind practiced in the U.S., is the customized, American version of the Japanese minimalism, the authentic approach to living a minimalistic life. Western minimalism can help you derive many of the benefits we have discussed, but it also has flaws.

In the next chapter, we shall delve deeper into the differences between the two and detail how the American approach to minimalism keeps you from reaping the full benefits of Japanese minimalism.

3.

WHY JAPANESE MINIMALISM IS THE BEST

Although minimalism seems like a relatively new term, it's an old term coined in the 1960s as a form of American Visual Art mostly associated with abstract design and expressionism.

Over the years, this term has made its way into the different aspects of Western living and somehow turned into a way of life that promises to help you live a simple, empowered life.

What most people don't know is that minimalism is a traditional Japanese concept, or that strict adherent of minimalism practices the Japanese style of minimalism, not the Western approach practiced in countries like Finland, Denmark, Britain, the U.S., etc.

As promised, in this chapter, we shall delve deeper into the differences between Japanese and Western minimalism, primarily focusing on illuminating why Japanese minimalism is the most authentic kind of minimalism—and why it's, therefore, the best kind of minimalism to adopt.

The Differences Between Western and Japanese Minimalism

The type of minimalism currently practiced in the Scandinavian countries and the U.S. mainly focuses on keeping whatever brings you joy and value. It revolves around the concept of keeping only that which adds comfort, convenience, and value to your life.

For instance, if you want to have a couch in your lounge, you get one—if you don't already have an adequate one—but if you have an old, torn futon that does not serve a purpose or add value to your life, you should get rid of that before getting the couch.

JAPANESE MINIMALISM

Western minimalism primarily focuses on decluttering your life by getting rid of the meaningless things, including anything worn out, useless, old, extra, and unnecessary, while keeping whatever adds joy, comfort, and value to your life.

For example, if you seek solace from your childhood stuff, Western minimalism dictates that you should keep the items. Western minimalism is more about assessing your needs, understanding what you truly need, and keeping anything, you need while discarding everything else.

It is not about getting rid of expensive or cheap stuff; it's about freeing yourself from things you don't need or that you bought after influence from media biases and consumerism, not because you genuinely need them.

For instance, if your MacBook adds value to your life because it helps you work better, you can keep it, but at the same time, you should sell or give out any extra laptop and related devices that you have but don't use.

Moreover, Western minimalism does not require you to strip your house, workspace, and different aspects of life free from everything. If a particular wall art brings you joy, you should put it up; if you can replace it with something more meaningful, you should go for it.

Japanese minimalism, on the other hand, roots in living a simple life and centers on the concept of *'less is more'*, without keeping anything beyond what you need to live a simple life. Japanese who choose to live a minimalistic life feel overpowered by the excess of things.

According to Japanese minimalism, consumerism results from conspicuous consumption, fierce competition, noise pollution, dehumanizing advanced technologies, and excessive greed. Those who practice Japanese minimalism do so out of a desire to break free from all this, which is why they opt for a simpler life, one where the only things they choose to keep in their lives are those they need, nothing more.

In a minimalistic American home, you are likely to see a couch or two, a coffee table, a few ornaments, and wall art.

JAPANESE MINIMALISM

If you walk into the home of a hardcore Japanese minimalist, you are likely to see a coffee table with a few cushions neatly placed around it, maybe a bonsai on the table, and only the required number of ceiling lights.

In a minimalistic American bedroom, you are likely to see a bed, a nightstand, a chair, and a few other belongings. In a minimalistic Japanese bedroom, you're likely to see a mattress only, and, in some cases, a chair.

JAPANESE MINIMALISM

Japanese minimalism is about Zen

The Japanese's penchant for living simple lives draws a lot of influence from Zen Buddhism. Zen, pronounced as 'ch'an', translates into 'meditation'.

Many of us consider meditation a practice that helps unlock inner peace. In reality, it is a state of being in complete peace and harmony with yourself.

As defined by adherent practitioners, meditation is not an act of doing; it's a state of being that you can achieve once you unite your body, soul, mind, and completely harmonize every aspect of your life.

Zen Buddhism is a determined, uncompromising, stripped-down, and cut-to-the-chase branch of Buddhism that does not believe in doctrinal refinements. It does not rely on any ritual, doctrine, or scripture. It spreads from one master to his/her disciple through personal, hard training.

In terms of lifestyle, Zen is about living in the moment and creating your reality by being true to yourself.

Instead of falling into the trap of wanting to be more or part of the rat race that yields no meaningful result, Zen is about slowing down so that you can experience each moment as it is to its fullest, a process that can help you find yourself.

A famous quote by Shunryū Suzuki, a Zen monk known for establishing the first non-Asian-based Zen Buddhist monastery, reads:

> *"Zen is not some kind of excitement, but concentration on our usual everyday routine".*

Zen is not about doing or being more; it's more about finding your true self and practicing it in every passing moment of life.

The fast-paced life most of us live doesn't do us any good. It only leaves us jumping from one task to another, always hoping to do and complete everything instantly. When you live like this, you are not living your life fully.

You turn into an automaton, a machine-like person that mechanically works on one task after another, robotically addressing everything that comes your way.

You don't stop to immerse yourself in the joy of the act of sipping your hot coffee or savor its warmth on your tongue. You ignore the beautiful smile on your baby's face and the coolness of the breeze that gently touches your face. Likewise, you don't recognize or acknowledge many of the little pleasure's life has to offer you every day.

A life characterized by rushing and jumping from one task to other leads to a monkey state of mind, a condition where your mind jumps from one branch of thought to the other.

Just as a monkey leaps from one branch to another, swinging the entire time, you swing from one activity to another. When you never pause enough to rest, you cannot find yourself or have the self-awareness needed to embrace the present moment.

Zen aims to help you break these shackles so that you can pause, slow down, reflect, and breathe for real. Japanese minimalism believes in that-: taking a break from all the chaos and noise around you so that you can relax, reflect, and find your true self. According to its precepts, you cannot do that when living in cluttered mental and physical spaces.

Marie Kondo, a renowned Japanese minimalist, and bestselling author who introduced the KonMarie style of decluttering, believes that physical clutter contributes to mental clutter.

She talks about how you can only find peace by uncluttering your life because when you rid your life of what's useless and valueless, you experience a sense of peace and calmness that helps you discover who you are.

Japanese minimalism is about keeping what You Need ONLY

Because it builds on the concept of Zen, Japanese minimalism is primarily about eliminating excesses from your life and mind.

Zen teaches the art of uncluttering your mind, being aware of your emotions, and maintaining a healthy mind and body connection so that you can create a harmonious life laced with joy.

To the Japanese, the best way to achieve this is by living a simple life; Japanese experts describe it as

'the waves of the ocean, tick-tock of the clock, and the warm rays of the sun'.

A simplistic, minimal life is about living as simply as possible, which means you don't need lots of couches, beds, nightstands, shelves, racks, ornaments, utensils, or light fixtures.

If you need to sleep, all you need is a mattress; a bed is optional. If you need to light up a room, you don't need a fancy light fixture or chandelier; a simple light fixed on the ceiling does the trick nicely.

If you live by yourself, you don't need a set of six plates and about a dozen spoons and forks; a plate, glass, one spoon, fork, and a knife is all you need. If you never sit on a chair, don't keep one. If you don't use a table, an empty room works just fine.

Japanese minimalism advocates for the concept of 'ma,' pronounced as 'maah', which refers to celebrating the space between things.

Ma is about voids, negative space, and emptiness. The Japanese integrate it into every aspect of life, including their gardens, architecture, music, poetry, floral arrangements, interior, activities, relationships, and the mind.

They believe that 'chi', the vital life force that flows through everything and is essential for our survival, can only flow when there are spaces for it to flow around, across, and between things freely.

JAPANESE MINIMALISM

If your house is full of unnecessary stuff, and your mind is home to worrisome thoughts, you won't have room for chi to flow in and around. When chi cannot flow freely, it experiences blockages, which causes emotional, physical, and health problems.

To allow the vital energy force to flow freely within you and your spaces, you need to create space for it, which means you should embrace the concept of 'ma'.

Instead of adding more stuff into your home and life, strip it clear of anything you don't need. The funny thing is that when you analyze things deeply, you will realize that you don't need much to live a happy life.

If you are never going to use paints, there is no need to buy them. If you wear perfume once in a blue moon, it is best not to purchase it at all. You don't need to fill every space and corner with stuff to beautify it. Real beauty comes from celebrating things as they are.

While American minimalism allows you to keep possessions you think bring you value, Japanese minimalism asks you to let go of all possessions that don't add value to your life because the truth is that you do not need them.

While a minimalist American home is likely to have a few books neatly organized on a shelf, a Japanese minimalist home won't have a bookshelf at all.

In a minimalist American home, you may see some wall art, ornaments, cabinets, and furniture; you are unlikely to see anything of nothing of that sort in a minimalistic Japanese space.

American minimalism allows you to have gadgets, electronics, and appliances; Japanese minimalism believes that if you don't use any of these things, you don't need them and should get rid of them—since they don't add value to your life.

In Japanese minimalism, instead of owning a slicer, use a knife to slice fruits and vegetables, and instead of having a few pots and pans, keep only one.

How Japanese Minimalism Can Help You Live A Better Life

Mari Kondo, the author of the New York Times bestseller book, *The Life-Changing Magic of Tidying Up*, and Fumio Sasaki, the author of *Goodbye, Things: The New Japanese Minimalism*, are the ones mainly responsible for popularizing the Japanese minimalist movement. However, Japanese minimalism is an old Japanese tradition that has helped many people attain clarity and peace.

The practice concentrates on the notion that all your material possessions will one day get stolen, lost, broken, sold, outdated, or tossed out. Because of this, it's nonsensical to cling on to any material possessions because once you start attaching yourself to material objects, you begin nurturing insatiable temptations and desires.

Desires, as Buddha said many thousands of years ago, only lead to pain and suffering. When you know that—and how—attachment and temptations will lead to suffering, the only logical and wise choice is to let go of everything that can breed attachment.

Japanese minimalism encourages you to let go of all your unnecessary desires gradually so that you can live with what you truly need. Western minimalism has a few loopholes, with the main one being the principle of keeping things that bring you value and joy.

For instance, if having a dining table adds convenience and comfort to your life, with Western minimalism, you can keep it in your house because it makes life easier for you. On the other hand, a Japanese minimalist would get rid of that—or swap a big table for a small one—and have food on a mat placed directly on the floor.

By allowing you to keep what you think is valuable and meaningful, Western minimalism somehow creates openings for desires, leading to attachment and suffering.

With Western minimalism, if you feel that the wall in your living room is empty, you are free to decorate it with a painting or two, just not too many of them as that would lead to a cluttered wall.

Through doing this, you would think of how a painting or a wall art would add color, value, and joy to the wall, and in return, create some attachment and meaning to the piece.

The wall art then starts becoming important to you, and, one way or another, you end up fearful of losing it. The 'want' to have wall art slowly leads to desire, attachment, and belonging, all of which lead to pain and suffering.

Likewise, every time you decide to keep a single item more than what you need, you create some opening for attachment, desire, temptation, and suffering in life.

In contrast, Japanese minimalism is free from such issues because it asks you to keep only that which you need, nothing extra at all. If you have a table, you don't need a decorative ornament. If you change clothes daily, you only need about 7 to 8 outfits, which means that instead of having two dozen outfits, you should regularly wash and clean what you have.

When you adopt it, gradually, the Japanese minimalist approach frees you from the desire to own and have more than you need. It helps you learn to live with a few things, and soon enough, those few items become enough. Slowly, you start appreciating the comfort, warmth, and convenience that comes with owning a few essentials.

When you do not have to worry about maintaining and cleaning lots of things, laundering piles of clothes, stressing about losing expensive items, and when you have less clutter in your house, you start to live, travel and move around with ease. This convenience feels like a unique luxury, one that you cannot find elsewhere.

Additionally, Japanese minimalism also teaches you how to let go of unnecessary thoughts, ideas, activities, and beliefs.

For instance, instead of always trying to be the best at everything or trying to do more just so you can stay at the top, you learn to pay attention to the real voice inside you. Being attentive to your inner desires and needs creates an inner awakening that helps you discover your true self and understand your genuine needs.

By being more attentive to your inner self, you start being more reflective of your thoughts, which helps you understand the root of different emotions and explore various things and ideas, thus allowing you to discover and understand yourself better. This ongoing process of self-discovery brings forth many realizations that help you make better life choices and pursue the things that matter the most to you in life.

Moreover, when you have fewer material possessions and meaningless things, your mind is less mentally cluttered, creating space for the free flow of energy. When energy flows freely in your mind, it creates space for meaningful thinking and makes it easier to figure out yourself better.

This awareness allows you to analyze the kind of relations you wish to keep in life, giving you a chance to free your life from negative influences. Gradually, you start letting go of everything and everyone that brings forth any suffering and toxicity in your life, which brings forth a newfound sense of harmony.

Western minimalism also advocates for this too. However, it cannot help you unlock all the benefits of the minimalistic approach, primarily because the former is full of loopholes.

It talks about letting go of unnecessary things, but at the same time allows you to keep what brings you joy, which creates openings for attachment. When you don't strip your life of everything but the basics, you won't find out what brings you pure joy and meaning.

Because Japanese minimalism advocates for detachment, it's the best approach to minimalistic living.

Now that you understand the distinct differences between Western and Japanese minimalism, we can start discussing how to adopt Japanese minimalism to make your way to enhanced harmony and complete empowerment.

The next chapter discusses one of the foundational principles of Japanese minimalism, the beautiful concept of **Wabi-Sabi**.

4.

WABI-SABI AND JAPANESE MINIMALISM

When your mug falls and chips, what do you do? If you're like most people, you probably throw it out and replace it with a new one, right?

Doing that feels like the natural thing to do because that cup now has an imperfection, looks old, and does not feel good enough to place on your kitchen shelves anymore.

On the surface of it all, throwing out a chipped cup is not wrong or unhealthy. However, on a deep level, there are flaws in doing so, something you realize the moment you analyze the situation a bit more deeply.

Not accepting imperfections can affect your life negatively

There is nothing wrong with discarding something old, shabby, and broken if it is useless and valueless.

If you have a rickety chair that does not serve the purpose for which you bought it, it makes no sense to keep it—keeping it otherwise borders on hoarding.

On the other hand, if the only thing wrong with the chair is that it has one broken leg, instead of investing money in a new one, you should repair and start using it again.

Here's the thing, unless you have a genuine need to purchase something new, doing so is useless, and replacing old things with new ones only promotes consumerism because it causes you to give in to the desire to have something new and attractive in your house.

The tendency to discard everything that looks and feels flawed and imperfect affects more than your buying behavior; it directly impacts your thought process as well.

When you start to find imperfections and flaws in old, shabby-looking things in your home, you also tend to focus your attention on what you consider personal imperfections. You start looking for flaws in your personality, weaknesses in your abilities, and deficiencies in your appearance. Suddenly, your nose seems too crooked, arms too flabby, and little-by-little, you start belittling yourself and gradually eroding your self-esteem.

When you belittle yourself, you start noticing different flaws in your routine life: A job you loved starts feeling menial; a car you loved starts looking old and out of date, and friends who once made you smile start feeling same-old same old.

Remember that it's one thing to analyze your genuine needs and make changes to your life accordingly, and an entirely different thing to find inadequacies in every aspect of yourself and your life—and feel bad about it.

The latter pattern of thought is harmful to your wellbeing because it makes it impossible to feel comfortable in your skin and nurture contentment for what you have.

Hedging against this is where Wabi-Sabi comes in: Wabi-Sabi is a popular Japanese concept that aims to make your life easier and more enjoyable by helping you embrace the imperfections in you and around you.

Once you learn to appreciate things, people, and yourself despite limitations and inadequacies, you find solace in what you have and stop pursuing the desire to have and be more. This fact is why Wabi-Sabi is the root of Japanese minimalism.

This chapter explores the concept of Wabi-Sabi further so that you can understand how it connects to Japanese minimalism and how to start infusing the two into your routine life.

JAPANESE MINIMALISM

The Beauty of Wabi-Sabi

The term Wabi-Sabi combines two brilliant concepts.

Both words (concepts) have individual, profound meanings, but when they marry, they bring about an all-embracing sense of warmth that you cannot find elsewhere.

Wabi

Wabi refers to *something peaceful that has intentional simplicity*.

At one point in Japanese history (14th-century), the term referred to simple Japanese monks who wore simple—sometimes tattered—robes, lived in simple houses, and went about their routine rituals without adornments of any kind. The Japanese considered them an epitome of simplicity and revered them for their unfussiness.

Over the years, Wabi has become associated with humility, austerity, and minimalism. The Japanese refer to people who exemplify a profound understanding of who they are—and who feel comfortable with that—as "Wabi".

Sabi

Sabi refers to *the subtle elegance of a person or object*, and while mostly applied to things, its connotation applies to people as well.

The whiskering on your old pair of jeans, the greenish hue of oxidation on the stunning Statue of Liberty, and that dark seasoning on the old skillet in your kitchen are all "Sabi".

Buddhism believes that something attains the element of Sabi with time as it ages and acquires different kinds of physical qualities that the outside world views as "imperfections", but that adds to the item's grace and sophistication. Hence, Sabi is a quality earned over time.

Wabi-Sabi together

When you combine the two terms, Wabi-Sabi refers to *a humble, gracious, and unfussy existence* based on fully comprehending and embracing yourself as well as the truth of impermanence. That best representation of this is in all the things that accept the misfortunes—or fortunes—of time and embrace them with untiring grace and dignity.

In terms of material possessions, you see Wabi-Sabi in the different imperfections that serve as evidence of wear and tear and gradual usage of that item.

Well-used things, especially those kept well and cared for, can never be mistaken for new things because the former have a special uniqueness that distinguishes them from other items, which is what makes them special.

Wabi-Sabi is clear to see on the face of the scuffed, worn-out shoes you own and keep at a special place in your closet. It's also what gives the chipped plate that your grandmother gave you and that you have eaten from for over ten years its uniqueness. That's the essence of Wabi-Sabi: *graceful, aged uniqueness.*

Wabi-Sabi is more than a mere concept; it's a way of life that allows you to appreciate complexities in life while valuing simplicity.

In his book, *Wabi Sabi Simple: Create beauty. Value imperfection. Live Deeply,* Richard R. Powell states that Wabi Sabi operates on the foundation of three simple fundamentals of life:

> *"Nothing ever lasts, nothing is ever finished, and nothing can ever be perfect".*

These three concepts allude to the three truths but often understated realities of life.

First, nothing is permanent. Change is the only constant thing in life, and to make any progress, you must acknowledge and accept change as the only permanent thing in life; everything else is temporary.

Understand and accept that life challenges are inevitable, and, therefore, to be happy, you must accept whatever you experience in the here and now.

Second, nothing ever ends because life goes on, and something that may seem useless to you can be incredibly valuable to someone else. You may be ready to discard a tattered T-shirt, but the same ragged tee can provide adornment to someone else who hasn't worn a tee in a long time.

We are the ones who attach terms such as "useless" to things, but in reality, nothing ever ends; all it does is turn into something else.

You need to develop a knack for seeing the good in everything, and in every situation, always look for what's valuable.

Third, nothing can ever be perfect because perfectionism is a myth.

You may consider your new mahogany coffee table perfect only for a friend to place a blue, ceramic vase on it and declares it perfect now. For you, the new black tuxedo you bought may look perfect until someone points out how there needs to be another button on the jacket.

There is—and always will be—some room for improvement in everything. When you chase perfection, you invite nothing but chaos and madness into your life because the pursuit of perfection is never-ending, and as long as you try to perfect things, you will never settle for what you have.

When you pursue perfectionism, you will never find anything to value about the present moment, which means you'll never feel content with yourself or your life. That may seem alright right now, but if you look deep within yourself, you will realize that living a life based on such a perspective is a recipe for life-long unhappiness.

Wabi-Sabi invites you to be happy in the present

The Wabi-Sabi way of life does not require you to have an abundance of wealth, incredible training, or extraordinary skills to be happy.

All it asks is that you have a mind that is accepting and quiet enough to acknowledge the muted elegance in the daily elements of life, and the courage to welcome everything as it is without trying to adorn it with added embellishments. Wabi-Sabi roots in the ability to relax, slow down, and transition from doing a lot to merely being in the moment.

When you start acknowledging the beauty in every moment you experience, you stop trying to change things and fighting every obstacle. Instead, you let things be, and with that, you start to flow with the present moment.

If you find out that your preferred airline canceled your flight to Washington at the last minute because of a blizzard, you stop lamenting about the setback. Instead of worrying about how this disrupts all your plans, you relax and think of the best way to utilize the extra time you now have.

If your son tripped over a cable and ended up breaking a pile of your favorite China plates, you do not yell at him for being sloppy, thereby causing the accident.

You acknowledge the loss, but at the same time, you choose to embrace it and perhaps use that as an opportunity to spend time with your son, using the broken pieces of China to create a unique collage.

Wabi-Sabi applies to more than finding joy and comfort in the routine life situation; it also relates to accepting yourself wholly, just as you are, which means you stop trying to be perfect or killing yourself to fix your flaws.

When you embrace the concept, you accept all your weaknesses as a part of who you are as a unique person and nurture a positive attitude towards everything that makes you, well, uniquely YOU. That, however, does not mean you do not work on self-improvement; you do.

It just means that when you realize you are a procrastinator; you do not criticize yourself for procrastinating. Instead, you encourage yourself not to postpone essential tasks, while at the same time accepting that sometimes, it's okay not to do a lot all the time.

JAPANESE MINIMALISM

Instead of criticizing yourself for being chubby and not working out much, you embrace your body as it is. From this positive frame of mind, you analyze your lifestyle and gradually make positive changes that will enable you to become healthier.

Kintsugi is a brilliant example of Wabi-Sabi in art and creativity. In this type of art, artists fill cracked pots with gold lacquer to enhance the beauty of the cracks and portray them as an element of aged, timeless beauty. Instead of hiding the cracks, the gold lacquer highlights it, adding to its graceful beauty.

Similarly, Wabi-Sabi aims to make you comfortable with all the cracks, damages, setbacks, falls, and errors you experience in life so that you can enjoy the wisdom, knowledge, and grace that comes with that.

Wabi-Sabi and Japanese minimalism share a unique and beautiful bond that aims to help you feel internally empowered.

Let us explore that bond before we move on and start discussing ways to implement Wabi-Sabi so that you can start living a minimalistic lifestyle.

The Unique Bond Between Wabi-Sabi and Japanese Minimalism

Japanese minimalism is about accepting the concept of *less is more* and uncluttering your life of everything valueless, even if that's your iPhone or Tesla.

The truth is that you don't need all that much to be happy and abundant. Wabi-Sabi talks about embracing imperfections and accepting things as they are without trying to perfect them.

When you incorporate Wabi-Sabi into every aspect of your life, you start finding joy and beauty everywhere, even in the old, worn out and seemingly useless stuff.

For example, the old couch you wanted to discard suddenly stops seeming so worn when you remember all the beautiful memories your partner and you have had on it. When you start perceiving the juice stains on it as mementos from your kid, the couch suddenly becomes very important for you.

Even if you were thinking of discarding that couch for a new one that costs $2,000, the instant you apply Wabi-Sabi to it, it stops seeming worthless after all, and you decide to keep and love it instead of getting a new couch that increases your expenses.

Similarly, you may feel that you need to buy twenty cups because you now have more guests and entertain more. However, when you think things through in light of Japanese minimalism and Wabi Sabi, you realize that not everyone drinks tea and that the three cups you have will be enough.

That's the beauty of Wabi-Sabi: Slowly and gradually, it gives you the courage to feel comfortable with whatever you have and find joy in it.

As this becomes your core belief, out of realizing that whatever you have right now is your best, you start to let go of the need to have more or the best of everything.

Likewise, when you apply Wabi-Sabi to yourself, you start feeling comfortable in your skin and letting go of the need to beautify yourself with mass-produced goods.

Your peppered hair starts to look good, your wrinkles feel like medals of your hard work, and the creases that form around your mouth when you smile stop being signs of aging and become what they are: tales of a joyous life.

When you embrace such a mindset towards your life, you stop buying too many cosmetics, looking for cuts and styles that make you look younger, and trying to use accessories to enhance your beauty. You accept yourself as the beautiful person you are, just the way you are.

As you can see, the Wabi-Sabi's way of living is peaceful, which is why it's able to keep you from falling prey to the rat race and rampant consumerism. Freedom from these two things is a monumental achievement because when consumerism, media biases, and societal stereotypes stop ruling our life, you can live free.

When you're free from the claws of consumerism, you realize that you don't need the latest LED TV to enjoy watching TV.

You realize that buying expensive perfumes is unnecessary because wanting to do so was never a real need, just a meaningless desire enforced by media-driven consumerism.

Freedom from consumerism allows you to detach from unnecessary desires and makes it easier to experience a happy, content life free from attachment-driven suffering.

Having explored the interconnectedness of Japanese minimalism and Wabi-Sabi and how the two can help you create a truly free life, let's discuss how to embrace these concepts and make them part of your daily life.

The 7 Principles to Help You Adopt Wabi-Sabi and Japanese Minimalism

Zen philosophy teaches seven principles that can help you achieve a Wabi-Sabi state of life that embraces concepts of Japanese minimalism.

To become a practicing Japanese minimalist, you must work on the seven principles of:

1. *Kanso*
2. *Fukinsei*
3. *Shibumi*
4. *Shizen*
5. *Yugen*
6. *Datsuzoku,* and
7. *Seijaku*

#1: Kanso

Kanso means simplicity or living a simple life.

Japanese minimalism tethers on the idea of living a simple life as the ultimate way to remove fuss or drama in your life. When you start feeling content with whatever you have, you find joy in the understated pleasures of life, which is when you achieve Wabi-Sabi.

Simple living (Kanso) is more challenging than it sounds, yes, but to a committed heart, anything is possible.

To infuse Kanso into your life, you need to make a few changes to the way you think and live.

How to infuse Kanso into your life

Here is what you need to do.

Step 1

First, analyze your current state of life and focus more on anything that may be raising your stress levels. For instance, reflect on the chaos, mismanagement, and lack of organization in your daily routine, and how this keeps you from being happy.

As you dig deeper into issues, you'll realize that most of the stress in your life ties back to owning—or trying to have—more stuff or trying to do more daily. When you analyze the situation under this light, you'll feel motivated to adopt Japanese minimalism and Wabi-Sabi for good.

Step 2

Next, think about how living a simpler life would improve the overall quality of your life.

Write down all the improvements you can think of, including enhanced inner peace, quality time with loved ones, contentment with what you have, and saving money. Elaborate each reason so that you gain a better understanding of how simple living would benefit you.

These reasons are the compelling WHYs that will give you the motivation you need to pursue your goal.

Every goal you set in life must have a compelling reason(s) why you wish to achieve it. These reasons help you keep going when facing challenges and setbacks.

The same applies to minimalism. Hence, the reasons (WHYs) you jot down now will give you the strength to fight back consumerism-driven urges and compulsions.

Step 3

Create copies of your list of compelling WHYs and put them up in different areas of your home and workplace. Every time you move past your fridge or sit on your work desk, you will glance at these WHYs and acknowledge your commitment to become a minimalist.

Step 4

With this newfound motivation to live a no-fuss life, apply the concept of Danshari in your life, which is a beautiful Japanese concept centered on 'uncluttering' and founded on three principles: *refuse*, *dispose*, and *separate*.

To implement Danshari, start doing the following:

- *Refuse:* Start by refusing any extras things you receive. Don't take free caps, mugs, T-shirts, perfume testers, ketchup sachets, and any such thing offered to you by marketers at malls and stores. Additionally, say a kind no to unnecessary gifts or keepsakes given to you by a loved one or anyone else in your social network. When you visit a potential client who then offers you a mug from his company's merchandise, politely refuse. If you feel refusing any present offered may hurt the sentiments of the person offering it, accept the gift, but pass it on to someone who needs it as soon as possible. Whenever someone visits you and offers to bring something, ask for what you need, and if you don't need anything, politely thank the person and then ask the person not to bring anything.

- *Dispose of:* Now start analyzing the different spaces in your home, looking for unnecessary stuff that you can dispose of —or let go. Start with items that have lost their meaning and value, or that you bought because they caught your fancy. Here, it is vital to highlight that you can toss out any old or broken stuff, especially those that don't serve any purpose. If you have a few couches, but you only use one, get rid of the rest. However, if you have just one old couch, and you plan to replace it with a new one, think about the memories held by the ragged cushions. If you feel like keeping it, do so, but if you wish to dispose of it, get rid of it.

- *Separate:* Thirdly, start separating what's important from what's not so that you can slowly unclutter your house and free it from meaningless things.

Step 5

Once you regularly embrace refusing, disposing of, and separating things in your home and workspace, you slowly begin to eliminate many things from your life. From this point on, your job is to keep up with this practice, love, and care for whatever remains in your spaces.

If your room, once filled with an iron stand, three chairs, a nightstand, a bed, and tens of cushions, now only has a bed, a chair, and an iron stand, find joy in all these items. If you keep telling yourself how less is more, soon enough, you will start believing it.

Step 6

Moreover, start looking for simpler alternatives to extravagant things in life. If earlier, leisure time meant dining out in an expensive restaurant, start cooking at home and invite a good friend over, or have a candlelight dinner with your partner on the patio. Similarly, if you used to go to the movies every Friday with friends, invite them over for a movie at home.

Generally, look for ways to cozy up with loved ones, or even spend quality time with yourself without always spending money or buying something extravagant.

At first, and to ensure you stay the course, take things slow. Take the plunge because taking action is the only way to achieve anything, but don't go overboard by instant simplification too far. Instead of tossing out all the furniture in your house, let go of one unnecessary piece every few weeks so that the transition is smooth and easier on you.

#2: Fukinsei

Fukinsei refers to the element of *irregularity*, which means you need to accept the irregularities in life and stop chasing perfectionism.

Nothing can ever be perfect because nothing has the potential to be completely right.

The flaws in every situation and our personality make us unique. You can only embrace true Wabi-Sabi when you become comfortable with the setbacks in life, start adjusting to normal irregularities and problems and stop desiring for more and better-seeming alternatives.

For example, you may wish to have a car because it's a convenient way of commuting compared to traveling on the bus or subway. However, when you think of how the long commute to work on a bus gives you a chance to meet new people, and how it removes the worry of having to drive a car, the latter option feels nicer, and you should accept it wholeheartedly.

Similarly, if you feel annoyed every time you plan a vacation and some contingency or mishap happens, think of the beauty of the moment that is, the *present*. Whatever you have right now is the only reality; everything that did not happen for you was never meant to happen for you. There's no point in remaining upset over things that never occurred.

To embrace Fukinsei in life, work on the following areas:

- Every time you experience a setback in life, understand that it happened because that's what should be. The only thing in your control is your thoughts and actions; everything else falls in the category of 'outside factors beyond your control. If you left for work on time but still got stuck in a traffic jam, that is not on you, and even if it was your fault, it happened. What's the point in worrying about it now?

- Whenever you encounter a problem, stop focusing on why it happened, or how you could have averted it. Instead, think of the lessons it teaches you and possible ways you to fix the problem. If you forgot to take your wallet and now you have no money to buy lunch, it is okay to feel upset, yes, but think of how this experience has taught you to check whether you have what you need before leaving home. Also, use it as an opportunity to be thankful for the times when you fed well and think of the plight of all those who are not as lucky to eat three or more times daily.

- Instead of finding people to blame for the irregularities in life, take accountability for your actions; it will help you become more self-assured and stronger.

- Moreover, every time you have an accident, say your son spilling juice all over the floor, or your partner forgetting to make dinner on time, don't get upset. Instead, use that as an opportunity to do something together with your loved ones. You and your son could clean the spillage together, or you could enjoy the process of preparing dinner together for a date night with your partner.

True minimalism comes from acknowledging the little joys in life. Often, those joys come from embracing the setbacks and irregularities in life because when you do, you stop wanting to be somewhere else, which makes it possible to live in and enjoy the here and now.

#3, #4, #5: Shibumi, Shizen and Yugen

Shibumi refers to the beauty in the understated things in life; Shizen stands for naturalness without any pretense, and the simplest translation of Yugen is subtle grace. Since the three principles have a very close relation, it's best to discuss them as one.

Wabi-Sabi is about finding beauty in the routine, understated, and apparent unattractive experiences or things in life. This beauty is without any pretense; it has a natural, subtle grace that makes it stand out from the rest.

The best way to acknowledge the elements of Shibumi, Shizen, and Yugen in your routine life is to start appreciating the grace in mundane experiences, old objects, and seemingly ugly things.

Your old bedspread with wrinkles on one corner and faded color on the other may seem worthless to you, but if you notice how that faded color has a unique grace to it, and how it still serves its purpose, you will start to appreciate it more.

Before discarding anything and replacing it with something new, look for the aspects of Shibumi, Shizen, and Yugen. Moreover, endeavor to accept, respect, appreciate yourself because you can only be happy with your life if you feel happy with yourself.

To make adopting these three principles seamless, work on the following aspects:

- Every day, spend a few minutes by yourself, acknowledging your inner and outer beauty and reminding yourself of how you feel comfortable in your skin. Say positive things such as, "I love myself", "I embrace myself as I am", "I accept myself wholeheartedly", and use other such positive statements. Such suggestions rewire your mind to think with positivity, which can help you stop looking for ways to perfect yourself and falling in the traps of the cosmetics and beauty industries.

- Think of the different unhealthy beliefs you nurture towards your body, and work on improving them. Instances of body shaming and a lack of self-acceptance can create mental assumptions that foster self-hate. Analyze the different parts of your body you don't seem to like much and think of how you look good the way you are. Reflect on the importance of every part of your body and use that to embrace and appreciate yourself. At the same time, practice positive affirmations that help you love yourself and remind you to take healthy measures to care of your body better. For instance, if you despise your chubby thighs, you could say, "I accept my thighs the way they are", and "I eat healthily and exercise every day so that I can stay fit". Such suggestions encourage you to practice self-love and live a healthier life.

- Think of your weaknesses and strengths, jot them down, and accept both as a part of who you are. If the need arises, work on overcoming your weaknesses without criticizing yourself. Doing this helps you become a better person from a place of positivity.

As you work on these areas, you will start settling in and enjoying the present moment as it comes and no matter what it presents. Moreover, you will begin to like yourself better, which will make it easier to find pleasure in mundane life experiences.

#6 & #7: Datsuzoku and Seijaku

Datsuzoku refers to freeness, while Seijaku translates to tranquility. You need both these elements to create peace, harmony, and balance in life. In essence, that means you need to unlock your free spirit and stop trying to live by a specific code that limits your life.

You should have rules and principles and abide by a core value system that helps structure your life in the desired manner. However, that does not mean you should confine yourself to living a certain way, especially one that makes self-experimentation impossible.

We all want tranquility in life. Unfortunately, very few of us realize that serenity comes from within. You feel calm when you allow yourself to breathe and live as you feel like, and when you stop limiting how to live and whom to be.

Embracing inner serenity allows you to be free. Once you feel still and tranquil from within, you stop seeking joy in having more stuff, buying extravagant things, and achieving colossal victories.

To embrace the principles of Datsuzoku and Seijaku, and, in so doing, start experiencing inner tranquility and freeness, start paying attention to your genuine inner needs. Think of what you genuinely wish to do, and if that brings you happiness, pursue it without hesitation.

For instance, if you don't want to work at a 9-5 job because you do not need that much money to be happy, quit the job, or, if possible, switch to a part-time option. If you feel like hitch-hiking your way to a new city just for the sake of adventure, don't let anything stop you. Allowing yourself to have different experiences in life gives you a chance to unleash your true, free spirit.

Once you start implementing these seven principles, you will notice a phenomenal increase in spiritual growth, inner peace, and a sense of deep contentment. You will begin to feel lighter, more relaxed, and energized.

Instead of being in a rush to do everything, you will learn to slow down while tending to important tasks and enjoying routine experiences more. Moreover, you will fall in love with yourself, which is one of Wabi-Sabi's primary goals.

The process of adopting these seven principles helps you nurture a more peaceful and mindful state of mind. This state of mind is essential to practicing Japanese minimalism because:

When you think clearly, you can distinguish between what sparks joy and what does not and can intentionally eliminate the latter to make more room for the former.

Having discussed the core principles of Japanese Wabi-Sabi, let's move on and discuss the KonMari method of uncluttering your house and life.

5.

THE MOST EFFECTIVE KONMARI DECLUTTERING TECHNIQUE: TIPS & HACKS

The KonMari Decluttering Method is a popular decluttering technique created by the renowned Japanese minimalist and cleaning consultant, Marie Kondo, famous for her bestselling book: *The Life-Changing Magic of Tidying Up: The Japanese Art of Decluttering and Organizing.*

The KonMari method is one of the most effective, minimalism-inspired ways to declutter your house by tackling all your belongings in a category-by-category manner instead of room-to-room.

The KonMari approach is not synonymous with Japanese minimalism. Yes, the process draws inspiration from the latter, but the two are not the same thing. That said, the KonMari technique can help you move closer to adopting Japanese minimalism.

In this chapter, we shall discuss everything you need to know about the KonMari Method, including hacks and tips you can use to apply the approach in the most effective way possible.

The KonMari method and Japanese Minimalism: The Link

The KonMari approach is about living with items that spark joy; on its part, Japanese minimalism is primarily about living with fewer things.

What many of us often fail to realize is that only a few things spark pure joy within us.

You may feel excited about holding a new iPhone, but if you look deep within, you may realize that your books are what spark that inner joy.

You may feel glad to have ten dresses in your wardrobe, but upon further consideration, realize that you only wear one of those the most because it makes you feel good.

You can know which items spark real joy within you once you eliminate clutter from your spaces. Once you start paying attention to the feelings stirred by different things, and the sentiments they cause, you can distinguish between meaningful and meaningless objects better.

The ability to distinguish between what matters and what doesn't help you comprehend how meaningless items eat away at your peace and joy, thereby making it easier to do away with them for good. The more you eliminate what's nonessential from your life, the easier it becomes to learn how to live with the few items that bring you pure happiness.

Worth noting here is that: You are free to use any decluttering method you want; the crucial thing is to eliminate excesses from your life and spaces. That's the goal!

However, since the KonMari approach has worked well for many people, particularly those who follow Japanese minimalism, it's the method we shall focus on and learn how to use effectively.

Basic Guidelines to Help You Master the KonMari Method

Like every approach that helps you arrive at a particular outcome, the KonMari method has some rules—consider them guidelines.

To achieve phenomenal results with the method and live your life like an authentic Japanese minimalist, you need to understand and follow these guidelines.

Here they are:

#1: Commit to tidying up

The first KonMari Method decluttering rule or guideline is to commit to the approach and goal.

Commitment is an essential core value that you must have before you can become an authentic Japanese minimalist—and fulfill all your other goals. When you commit fully to a cause, you never give up on it no matter how many odds stack up against you. Similarly, you need to commit to tidying your entire home and every space you wish to clear and declutter.

Adopting Japanese minimalism improves your life and overall wellbeing, yes, but at first, taking it up is challenging and overwhelming. Even if you take things slow, you will experience instances where you struggle to part with some sentimental, but nonessential objects. If you commit yourself to the goal, your commitment will remind you of the importance of what you are doing and why you are doing it in the first place.

Moreover, when your commitment is strong, you will do everything you can to eliminate any unwanted object in any part of your house to keep it clutter-free and organized. Commitment ensures you don't allow meaningless stuff to enter your space and keep it tidied up.

#2: Visualize your dream lifestyle

Thinking of your ideal lifestyle often keeps you aware of how exactly you wish to live your life.

In his book, *You 2: A High-Velocity Formula for Multiplying Your Personal Effectiveness in Quantum Leaps*, Price Pritchett talks about the importance of having a clear vision of your goal and how that is the secret to achieving anything.

We often worry about having the most foolproof plan when what we should be worrying about the most, especially if we want to achieve results, is our vision. Failing to get the vision right is one of the primary reasons why many of us never achieve the results we want in life.

If you wish to achieve phenomenal success, first, what you wish to accomplish must be clear long before you think about the process that takes you towards it. Once your goals are 100% clear, you feel internally compelled to achieve them, which drives you to find a way to make it all happen. The same principle applies to uncluttering your life and spaces the Japanese way:

You need to figure out your ideal lifestyle and imagine living that dream as vividly and as often as possible.

Think of how you wish to feel relaxed in your life. Visualize your clean, organized rooms, and dream of the sense of peace and contentment you want. Think too of how all that is possible when you learn to live with things you cherish.

If possible, write about your ideal lifestyle in a journal or create audio logs detailing what you want. When you do this, you create a record of your dream lifestyle and can go through the written or audio logs repeatedly, thereby strengthening that imagination in your mind. The deeper your vision gets embedded in your head, the more you think about it, and the more driven you feel to achieve it.

#3: Be thankful for items before discarding them

The Japanese are incredibly humble people, and if you read about their culture and traditions, you will realize that deep humility and gratitude are some of their driving societal values. They believe that true contentment and peace comes from being thankful.

When you are thankful for something—or to someone—you acknowledge how that thing—or person—benefitted you. Even if you are parting ways with that object or person, you tend to do so in a kind, loving manner, without holding any grudges.

Distancing yourself from something or someone is usually a painful process. From living with that thing or person, you are likely to develop particular sentiments for it. Hence, when it comes to parting ways, all those feelings come flooding back in, making it difficult to let go.

If your sentiments are of joy and good memories, you struggle to say goodbye to them. If you harbor feelings of hate, pain, and negativity for that item or person, you don't struggle much; you can let go easily, but often with grudges.

When you train yourself to thank everything and everyone before letting go, parting ways becomes easier. Even when parting ways hurts a little, since you do it on a positive note of gratitude, you feel happy about the departure. That is why the KonMari method and Japanese minimalism ask you to thank every item for serving its unique purpose in your life before parting ways with it.

Every time you decide to eliminate an object from your house, hold it close, think of all the ways it benefitted you or added value to your home, and acknowledge its purpose.

For example, if you are getting rid of a cushion, think of how it made your couch look cozier and gave you comfort every time you rested your head on it.

Say, *"Thank you for giving me comfort. I am now ready to part ways with you so that you can add comfort to someone else's life"*. You don't necessarily have to say it out loud; you can silently say it in your mind too. However, saying it out loud often leads to a more profound sense of gratefulness for the item.

When getting rid of a specific item in your home, before thinking about discarding it, first focus on giving it to someone else who might need it. Yes, if the thing appears incredibly worn out or completely broken, discard it, but if you feel someone can use it, it is best to donate it.

#4: Tidy by category

When we declutter our spaces, we often follow the conventional room-to-room approach. For example, you are likely to declutter your entire bedroom, followed by your kitchen, lounge, bathroom, and other rooms of the house.

While this approach may work for you, if you analyze it deeply, you will realize that somehow, it leaves certain items untouched, and sometimes, other things tend to make their way into your house. That happens primarily because of the shortcomings of the room-to-room approach.

Every room tends to house many types of items. For instance, your bedroom will have some books; some magazines will be in the lounge, with some storybooks in your kids' bedroom.

When you practice the room-by-room approach, there is a high chance you may forget to get rid of a magazine lying in the drawer of your coffee table. You may get rid of a few books from your bedroom, but not all, hoping to set them all on a shelf in your study, something that never happens.

A better way to unclutter your space is to move category-by-category:

The KonMari approach notes that when it comes to decluttering, there are five primary categories to address:

1. *Clothes*
2. *Books*
3. *Papers*
4. *Miscellaneous—Komono in Japanese—items*
5. *Sentimental items—items that hold great sentimental value*

As you declutter your house, you need to sort items into these categories, and then instead of moving from one room to another, work on uncluttering the categories.

This approach allows you to tackle all the items in a category. When you work on a category, you rummage for items belonging to it in every room instead of just sticking to one space.

When you take this approach, you move through all the rooms, nook, corners, and storage spaces in your house that may be hiding any item from any category, take it out, analyze its importance, and then discard it.

#5: Follow the order of the rules/guidelines

It's vitally important that you work on these guidelines in the same order outlined here.

First, commit yourself to the cause, followed by imagining your dream lifestyle, thank every item for serving its purpose in your life when discarding it, and move from one category to another, sticking to the order of categories as well.

The order you should use to declutter different categories requires you to declutter your clothes first, followed by books, then papers and miscellaneous items, and lastly, sentimental items.

#6: Figure out if an item brings you joy

When getting rid of an item from your space, ask yourself if it genuinely sparks inner joy. Instead of discarding an old jewelry box, hold it close to your heart—literally—and ask yourself if that box still brings you any joy or if you cherish it in any way.

If the answer is yes, keep the item a bit more, and analyze your feelings for it after a few more days. After a few days, if you still feel the same about it, keep it. However, if that item no longer resonates with you, it means it has now served its purpose, and that you are ready to move on and let go.

Here are tips you should practice when implementing this guideline:

- Analyze the importance and value an item adds to your life. For instance, if you are about to discard a pair of loafers, think of how the shoes sheltered your feet and helped you look good on many occasions.

- While doing that, try not to let sentimentality carry you away. Remember that there are differences between feeling connected to an object because it sparks pure joy inside you, and just thinking of its purpose in your life and getting carried away with it. If you like a blouse you've had for five years but now feel it is time to give it away, don't let sentimentally keep you from doing so.

- For every individual item you intend to keep, think of how you plan to use it. If you are thinking of getting rid of a few towels but are having second thoughts, think of the purpose they will serve in the future. If they will only aimlessly lie in the closet, it is best to give them away.

Keep this step-in mind when uncluttering the different categories.

The Ultimate Category-by-Category Decluttering Plan

Here is how you should unclutter each category:

#1: Clothes

- When decluttering your clothes, take out all the clothes you own and sort them in categories such as sweaters, T-shirts, blouses, skirts, undergarments, summer shorts, etc.

- With each category, look for clothes that don't spark a connection, and ask yourself if a particular pair of socks or a scarf still sparks joy. Your mind answers questions based on how you ask them. If you ask yourself why you need to keep a pair of sunglasses, you will get several reasons why it's special. This fact is why the KonMari approach requires you to ask yourself, *"Does this item spark joy"*? Asking yourself this question allows you to get a clear yes or no answer. If you don't feel like keeping a certain hat, you will get a clear answer about it. When you ask this question and get a "NO" answer, it is time to get rid of that object.

- As you reflect on whether you cherish a particular item, also think of whether it adds any sort of value to your life. In terms of clothes, value comes from their comfort, how good they make you feel, whether they still fit you and whether they suit your style and physique. If you have outgrown a pair of jeans and are not discarding it because it reminds you of your school days, consider whether it is a meaningful keepsake. If you feel you can live without it, that's your heart signaling that it's time to let go; don't hold on any longer!

- While decluttering your clothes, unclutter all your accessories and shoes as well. Make sure to toss out everything you have outgrown or don't enjoy anymore. If you have a scarf torn at an end, but you love it enough to sew the patch to continue using it, keep it. You can give away any new scarf or another clothing item you don't use or that doesn't add any meaning to your life.

- Discard all the things you have been saving for times when you lose or gain weight, more so those that don't spark a connection or joy.

#2: Papers

Papers are another massive category that encompasses everything from documents to journals to notebooks to utility bills to contact papers to wrapping sheets to every other type of paper you have in your house.

To unclutter this category, follow the guidelines below:

- Scan every corner and room of your house for any sort of paper item.

- Gather all paper-related items, and sort them into categories like work-related documents, personal documents, utility bills, tuition fee bills, etc.

- From every category, separate important documents from unimportant ones.

- From the categories of utility bills, personal and official documents, analyze the ones you need at any cost and should not discard. If you have old tickets, bills, passports, or other documents you are sure you won't require further, discard them.

- When discarding paper, shred the ones you have to discard—if you have a paper shredder. If you don't, you can burn what you don't need.

- Once you decide to keep some related paper items, observe your feelings for them for a few days, and if you don't use them or they don't spark any joy, you're better of getting rid of them.

#3: Books

This category includes books of all kinds such as magazines, coloring books, novels, magazines, academic books, activity books, and travel guides.

Here is how you should declutter things from this category.

- Give away all old books, magazines, journals, etc. to old bookstores, libraries, organizations, or individuals accepting such donations.

- Only keep the books, magazines, directories, journals, etc. that you need because they spark joy or add value to your life.

- Spend some time with every item you decide to keep and observe your feelings for it. Here, be honest with your emotions to ensure you only keep things that move you, not unnecessary clutter.

#4: Miscellaneous Stuff

This category encompasses everything else that does not fall into the categories mentioned above; things like utensils, cutlery, gadgets, electronics, appliances, decorative items, toiletries, cosmetics, etc. fall here.

Here's what you need to do:

- To unclutter this category, follow the guidelines above, and also pay attention to the functionality of every item.

- If an appliance does not work, and you haven't had it fixed in ages, it is best to get rid of it.

- If you have an appliance or gadget that does not work, but you no longer need it, discard it. If you have a potato peeler or slicer, but you have eliminated potatoes from your diet, there is no point in keeping that gadget.

- Gauge your sentiments for items you use, and do not let your temptations cloud your genuine feelings.

#5: Sentimental Items

This category includes all the items that hold any sentimental value and that you feel connected to in one way or the other.

For example, a sweater your grandma knitted for you is likely to have more sentimental value than a sweater you bought from a store. Gather all such items from all the categories discussed above and observe your sentiments for them.

Just hold the item close to you, and ask that million-dollar question: *"Does it move me in any way?"* If the answer is 'no,' you have no business keeping it: let it go!

Sometimes you need a few days to prepare yourself for this transition; take all the time you need but remember to do it eventually. If you are honest and conscious throughout the process, you will move forward at your pace.

Use these guidelines to de-clutter your home and other spaces.

KonMari Method Tips and Tricks to Help You Declutter Like a Pro

To ensure that the KonMari process works for you:

Keep three types of boxes with you at all times

Get boxes to add things to and label them *keep*, *discard*, and *donate* categories. You should have one box from each category with you every time you're decluttering so that whenever you find something worthless, or an item that doesn't spark joy, you can toss it in the discard or donate boxes.

Take things slow and steady

It is best to take a slow and steady approach to the process; don't try to declutter your entire house in one go.

The KonMari approach teaches that we should declutter everything in one go, which you can do. However, if this is your first time trying to adopt minimalism, trying to do everything in one take is likely to be emotionally exhausting, and you should not do it. Instead:

You could work on one category for a few days, and once done with it, move to the next category. Take some time between categories to relax and allow the new feeling to settle in before moving to the next category or even within a certain category.

For instance, if you have uncluttered a few items from the 'books' category, but notice a flare-up of temptations, stop for a few days, use the time to calm down, and then move forward.

Declutter the entire category first

Before moving to another category, make sure to declutter the current category you are working on until completion.

Declutter all your clothing items and accessories before you start working on the paper's category. If you jump between categories, you are likely to feel emotionally swamped and confused. You may also mix up a few items and somehow feel compelled to keep certain items. Because of this, it's wise to do away with all sorts of useless items from an entire category before moving to the next category.

Do it regularly

Decluttering is an ongoing process because, one way or the other, some clutter will creep into your spaces at one point or the other.

Moreover, your feelings about different things are likely to change over time as well. A crystal bowl you once loved may have lost its charm. A wallet that held great sentimental value last year may seem like junk now.

To ensure you do not keep any clutter, declutter your spaces regularly. It is best to dedicate a few minutes to every category daily, or if you have a hectic schedule, every few days. This way, it becomes easier to spot meaningless stuff on time and discard it before it forms deeper roots in your heart and life.

Organize and clean stuff

Uncluttering stuff is not enough because you can have a messy house with a few times scattered here and there.

The idea behind Japanese minimalism is to add value, joy, and meaning to your life. You start this journey by uncluttering your house, but you complete it by cleaning and organizing all your belongings.

Now that you have decided what to keep, clean every item from the 'keep' category, and then neatly organize everything at its rightful place—make sure you assign every item a fixed spot. It will make sure you have a specific location for everything.

When you keep things in an orderly fashion, at their fixed spots, you find them quickly, do not lose important things and do not have to wait hours to find something when you need it.

Moreover, dust, mop, and wipe your stuff regularly —at least 3 to 4 times a week—so that everything looks spick and span.

Dust and dirt trap the positive energy flowing around a space, limiting its ability to flow smoothly, thereby creating environmental imbalances that keep you from feeling truly happy.

Keep a journal

You need to track your minimalism journey so that you can know your performance, accomplishments, and setbacks.

When you declutter, journal about it, and include the time, date, and feelings towards the item and life in general before and after taking that action.

Additionally, observe your stress levels, and jot those down as well. Review your journal entries every week; it will help you gauge your performance and make changes accordingly.

<u>Be thankful for everything you have</u>

Stick to these guidelines, and make sure you are grateful for an item before discarding it. Once you declutter your living spaces, you will feel more relaxed and will be in a position to work on decluttering your professional life, which the next chapter shows you how to do.

6.

HOW TO APPLY JAPANESE MINIMALIS TO YOUR WORK AND PROFESSIONAL LIFE

By now, you understand that Japanese minimalism—and minimalism in general—does not have a strict code of rules you should follow to adopt a minimalistic lifestyle.

You also know that minimalism is about ridding different areas of your life of superficial and extra elements.

Given that, while the average person is likely to reduce minimalism to aesthetics and personal belongings, you can also apply its core principles to your work life.

Japanese minimalism allows you to consider and understand the complexities of things that occupy space in your life and mind, and then consciously simplify them. As a result, every area of your life becomes about embracing its most basic expression.

You can implement minimalism in your work and professional life, leaving a profound effect on these core areas. In this chapter, we shall discuss how to do this well.

Minimalism and Your Work Life

A quote by Joshua Fields Millburn and Ryan Nicodemus, proprietors of *The Minimalist*, a popular minimalism-based blog, reads,

JAPANESE MINIMALISM

> *"Minimalism is a tool to get rid of the excesses of life in favor of focusing on what is important so you can find happiness, fulfillment, and freedom".*

Minimalism can bring happiness, freedom, and contentment to your work life and career by encouraging you to get rid of everything that weighs you down or bring you joy.

When you analyze your work life, workload, and routine in an unbiased manner, and doing so does leave you smiling, it's clear that your career life is not giving you career satisfaction.

Your career is a core aspect of your life; you invest a lot of your time and energy into it per day. Most people have an 8 to 10-hour work routine.

If you add the time required to prepare for work, get ready, and return home after work, the time you direct to your professional life can amount to more than 13 hours.

If an aspect of your life consumes such a massive amount of time, space, and energy in your life, it needs to bring you happiness because if it does not, you will feel unhappy and dissatisfied with your life. When something drains you emotionally, mentally, and physically, it leaves you feeling miserable.

When your work does not feel fulfilling, you'll feel caged and never connected to or satisfied with what you do it. Even when you work every day, the only thing you're likely to have is complaints about your work life. You'll hate your boss; the nature of your work (job or business) will annoy you, and you will despise talking about your work. Such feelings do not stay limited to your work only; they also influence your wellbeing, fitness, health, and relationships.

Naturally, when you hate your work, you feel grumpy most of the time. You're likely to be irritable with your loved ones and prone to venting out your annoyance on them. Such a situation causes relationship rifts, leaving you feeling lonely and unhappy.

Irritability often causes us to make unhealthy choices—like binge eating as a coping mechanism, which is likely to affect your health negatively. If you don't stress-eat when you feel irritable and upset, you're likely to avoid eating, which can also decrease your emotional wellbeing.

To keep this from happening, you need to love your work, which minimalism can help you do in the following ways:

- Minimalism allows you to understand the core values, interests, and strengths pertinent to your work life. That understanding ensures you only engage in meaningful projects and activities. If you are a freelance graphic designer who recently ventured into content development, but the latter weighs you down, you let go of it.

- It also helps you understand the amount of workload you want to take and manage; this ensures you only work as much as you need to without overburdening yourself with more than you can handle. For instance, when you eliminate excesses from your home and let go of the need to have more, you realize you don't need a lot of money to live a simple, happy life. This realization helps you understand how a 6-hour work routine is sufficient to fulfill your basic needs, which means you can stop working for 10 hours daily and can, instead, use the extra time to relax and engage in things that fill your heart with joy.

- Not working round the clock saves you time, effort, and energy, consequently helping you feel calm, energized, and centered.

- You can use the additional time reflecting on your needs, bonding with loved ones, doing things you enjoy, and simply being in the moment.

- Moreover, minimalism encourages you to reflect on what you genuinely want to do and make changes to your work-life accordingly. For instance, perhaps you have always wanted to pursue a career in the food industry, not become a geologist. Since minimalism helps you understand the importance of embracing what and doing what brings you joy, in this case, you can find the inner courage to pursue your dreams. Doing this is likely to leave you experiencing joy, passion, and work-life fulfillment.

- A considerable benefit of minimalism is increased focus, productivity, and engagement. When you don't have scores of emails to respond to, phone calls to return, and a gazillion activities to carry out, your life becomes about what's essential. This simplicity allows you to engage in those tasks with increased focus and attention. With increased focus and concentration, you can grasp a task better, work on it, perform it well, and enjoy the process. When you don't have to do several tasks simultaneously, you engage better with the task at hand, and because you enjoy the process, you yield better results.

- Moreover, minimalism aims to simplify your work life by allowing you to plan things better and opt for useful tools you can use to complete tasks. You may come across an app that will enable you to create and streamline reports. As a result, you complete a task that used to take two to three hours in an hour. In this case, spending some time reflecting and planning things helps you come up with more effective ways of doing things.

- These changes also help you understand your priorities clearly, thereby ensuring you focus on only what matters and can enjoy your work better. Many people are already into professions they like, or that once brought them joy. Unfortunately, somehow, and with time, they feel disconnected from it. This lack of connection comes from not feeling excited about your work. Once you learn to slow down, take one task at a time and carry it singlehandedly and with complete focus, you automatically become more involved with everything you do, which helps you establish that long-lost connection with your work.

Minimalism can help you make these positive changes to your professional life, giving you a golden chance to love what you do and do what you love.

Steps to Help You Apply Minimalism to Your Professional Life

Here is how you can integrate minimalism into your career and professional endeavors:

#1: Reflect on your career

First and most importantly, reflect on your professional life and become intimately aware of what you want. Whether you are in a full-time job, a part-time one, or running a business, here are a few things you need to think about and clarify:

- Think of the core values you wish to use to shape your professional life.

- Ponder on your ambitions, dreams, and what you wish to do in your life in terms of your career. While doing this, go through your strengths, accomplishments, and skills to understand what you are good at and wish to do.

- Reflect on your current profession and determine whether it aligns with your values and ambitions. If you have always wanted to pursue a teaching career but are doing something else now, think of whether you feel connected to your current profession or wish to go back to what you want to do.

- Once you have a better understanding of the kind of career you wish to pursue, if you are not on that career path, think of how you can shift to it now. For example, if you have decided to establish an interior design company but are working in an accountancy firm right now, think about making a slow transition to what you want, especially if you cannot afford to lose your current job.

- If you decide to stick with your current profession, think of what about it pains you, and then determine how you can improve those issues. Perhaps you feel annoyed by a particular team member who nags you a lot, keeping you from enjoying your work. In that case, you could seek help from the HR department or ask your boss to assign you another team member. You could even talk to the team member in question and sort the issue.

- Moreover, think about your work hours and the kind of workload you wish to take. If you currently work for 12 hours, something that's taking a toll on your sanity and health, think about whether this is what you want, or whether you would like to decrease your work hours.

Every day, to understand what you want and how much you wish to work in that area, spend a few minutes reflecting on your career choices:

#2: Declutter your professional activities

With your professional ambitions, values, strengths, interests, and workload in mind, analyze all your professional activities and use this process to figure out the ones you wish to keep and eliminate. For example, if you are a journalist who pursued this profession to become a political journalist but somehow, you have shifted towards fashion journalism, something you find draining, ponder on it. Think of which of the two industries you wish to stay in and then commit to related projects.

Similarly, if your job responsibilities and tasks are more than what the fine print noted, which you find draining, talk to your boss regarding the issue. Discuss the problem openly and, together, look into offloading your activities. Start taking only as much work as you can handle and ensuring that you don't over exhaust yourself or experience burnout.

If you own and run a business, reflect on the type of projects you wish to take on, people you want to engage with, and ventures you want to pursue. For example, If you are a real estate agent who deals in commercial real estate, but you have now started a construction project that is draining your energy, think of whether you wish to pursue it or are better off doing what you love. If you are doing it to make more money, and it does not spark joy for you, it is best to disengage from it.

#3: Identify important tasks and prepare your To-do list

We usually feel swamped by our work because we don't prioritize our tasks, never have a planned schedule or an up to date To-do list to compliment it.

This discrepancy causes us to forget vital tasks, engage in meaningless activities first, and waste our time doing nothing productive. In the end, we feel more drained than before, getting nothing fruitful done, and find ourselves hating our work even more.

Simplify the problem by getting into the habit of planning your work the night before. Here are tips to help you:

- Considering your important upcoming projects, set your weekly targets.

- For every milestone, identify the list of activities you need to complete to achieve it.

- Of those tasks, differentiate high and low priority ones. High priority tasks are those that boost your productivity and help you achieve your targets faster. Low priority tasks are usually supportive tasks that help you progress through the day but don't always directly relate your professional milestones. For instance, preparing your business plan is a high priority task; when setting up your business, doing laundry first is a low priority task.

- Create a schedule accompanied by To-do lists for the day, and schedule your high priority tasks for earlier in the day or a time when you feel the most energetic. Doing this ensures that you complete difficult and crucial tasks first, or when you feel fresh, which increases your productivity.

- Analyze the importance of every task, the deliverables associated with it, and how it impacts your milestones. For example, if you have scheduled three meetings of 20 minutes each for the day regarding the same project, schedule one 30-40 minutes long meeting to discuss the entire project in one go. This way, you will 20 minutes and spare everyone the hassle of coming to the meeting room several times during the day.

- Go through your To-do list a few times to identify any nonessential tasks you may have listed on it. For instance, if you have planned to have a telephonic conversation with a potential client, but you can have the same conversation via email, opt for the more convenient and time-saving option.

- When planning your tasks, look for apps and tools that can help you execute a task faster and quicker, thereby simplifying the hassle and making the task more manageable.

As you start observing these guidelines, your work life will begin feeling more relaxed and impactful, all because you plan things and your time, and take up only as much as you need to and can handle without feeling overwhelmed.

#4: Overcome distractions

A successful minimalist has laser focus. He/she knows what he/she wants with clarity and how to distract himself/herself from everything that does not align with this. To enjoy your work better and improve your performance, you need to learn the art of defeating distractions.

Here are strategic ways to achieve that:

- Start working on tasks singlehandedly, or, in other words, **stop multitasking**. If you are preparing your pitch deck for a business competition, work on it only; don't check your email in between or browse through Amazon. Doing one task at a time frees your mind from unnecessary clutter, allowing you to give undivided attention to the important undertaking and become fully immersed, thereby understanding it well enough to perform better at it.

- Identify your distractions such as talking to friends, watching shows on Netflix, checking social media newsfeed, etc. and learn to say no to yourself every time you feel tempted to engage in such distractions.

- Additionally, make positive changes to your work environment by gradually eliminating all types of distractions. If your office has a bed-styled couch that makes you feel sleepy, distracting you from work, remove it.

- When working, put your phone and gadgets in silent mode and put them away.

- Turn off all app and gadget notifications to avoid distractions from constant beeps and the temptation to check your messages, emails, and social media newsfeed.

- Set fixed visiting hours and stick to them. Once you stop attending to guests and visitors during work hours, you'll be able to focus better on your work, leading to better, faster results.

- Remind yourself of the importance of achieving your targets, and whenever you embark on any work, visualize achieving what you're doing. Visualizing success motivates you to work with killer focus, helping you beat distractions.

As you follow these guidelines, track how you manage your distractions every day because it'll help you become more aware of your strengths and weaknesses.

Moreover, this approach also allows you to observe yourself closely enough to identify more distractions that may be keeping you from working effectively.

#5: Go on a digital detox

Although digital technologies have become an integral part of our routine lives and work, once in a while, go on a digital detox or cleanse to free yourself from the unnecessary need and temptation to use digital media.

Many of us fail at focusing on our tasks and enjoying them because of our addiction to screens—especially phones, T.Vs, and laptops.

Naturally, when you feel more interested in which of your friends vacationed in Paris or have more Snapchat followers and not on the business report you need to write, you will hate your work—and your productivity will be low.

Besides keeping you from actively doing your tasks, digital technologies also upset your time management.

When you become addicted to screens, you'll spend more time aimlessly surfing the web or browsing through someone's social media newsfeed than you do on completing productive, work-related tasks. Being in such a situation will make it impossible to complete your work on time, because of which you'll always feel emotionally swamped.

Moreover, if you closely observe your sentiments towards your work, you will realize that social media posts of someone's promotion, professional success, and enjoyable work-life are often the cause of hating your job and wanting more.

Even if you don't hate your job, when you see a social media post of a friend who works for a multinational firm enjoying a company-sponsored vacation in Hawaii while your firm never takes you on such excursion trips, you'll experience a pang of jealousy

You may not want to become a millionaire, but when you find out that a high school classmate many of you considered doltish is now the owner of multi-million-dollar companies, your desire for more money will flare-up.

Regular exposure to such compels you to compare your situation to others, and when you realize that your life does not seem as accomplished, it disturbs your inner peace.

Besides causing all these problems, continuous exposure to your phone, tablet, and computer screens harm your emotional and psychological wellbeing.

The blue rays emitted by these screens negatively impact your brain health by disrupting your circadian rhythm, your body's natural sleep-regulating clock.

When there's disharmony in your circadian rhythm, sleeping well becomes a challenge, and you start suffering from sleep-related problems.

Remember that mental clutter and chaos make it impossible to free yourself from excess workload and tensions, making it impossible to enjoy your professional endeavors.

A digital detox can help you avoid and overcome all this.

A digital detox is about consciously refraining from using digital technologies for some time, unless otherwise necessary. If your work depends on technology, you can use such technologies for work purposes only; you should not engage in them unnecessarily.

Here is how to implement a digital detox:

- Begin by slowly reducing the time you spend on social media platforms. On average, we spend 6 hours or more on our mobile phones every day, with a major chunk of that time spent on social media platforms. If you habitually check your Facebook feed after every few minutes, consciously close it every time you open the app. Observe your total exposure and usage of digital media technologies, and then intentionally reduce your usage by a few minutes at a time every day. If you realize you are on your phone for 7 hours a day, time yourself every time you use it, and consciously reduce your usage until you only use your phone for a few hours and eventually, for as little as possible each day—only when you need to really.

- Delete social media apps from your phone, one at a time. When you have to switch on your laptop every time to see who liked your latest profile picture, you will slowly feel less inclined to check your social media profiles time and again.

- When working, switch off your phone to remove the temptation of wanting to use it.

- Instead of watching movies online, or listening to music on YouTube, find other means to have leisure. To kill boredom and engage in healthy entertainment, go for walks, paint pictures, read books, etc.

- Dedicate a time window to using digital technologies, including web-based applications, browsing the web, and using social media. For instance, if you usually use digital media whenever you are on breaks, dedicate one hour, 5 PM-6 PM as your window to engage in digital media technologies.

- Do not use your phone or laptop while eating or when relaxing during your break hours. Eat and enjoy your meals without depending on technology for entertainment, which will thereby reduce your extreme dependence on it slowly and gradually.

- Once you build a habit of all these practices by consciously engaging in them, take a few days break from all types of digital technologies. You could take a few days off from work and use that time to unwind and re-energize without using any devices. If that isn't a feasible option right now, you could commit to not using digital technologies during your off days; just relax.

Once you go on a digital detox, you will feel its positive effects, and the anguish of doing so will be well worth it.

#6: Stop bringing your work home

Work starts being annoying when it becomes a full-time, inescapable part of your routine.

If your work hours never end, and you are always working, even when you are eating dinner with your family, you will become irritable and loathe your work life.

Letting work consume you is equivalent to bitting more than you can handle. This behavior paves the way for mood disorders and causes you to nurture negative sentiments towards your work.

The right way to remedy this issue is to stop bringing your work home. When your work hours end, you should stop working and prepare to go home for relaxation.

Entering your home should instantly relax you, not drain you or cause you to think about the piles of work you need to complete past your work hours. You need to change this so you can relax when you reach home, energize your body and mind, and feel ready to take on your tasks for the next day with increased zeal and zest.

Here are foolproof ways to do that.

- Ensure you have fixed working hours and set reminders that consciously encourage you to close your laptop and work when your work hours end.

- If you can, have a separate laptop for work-related tasks, and leave it at the office as you head back home. By doing this, you will not feel the urge to open it, check your emails, or complete any pending or incomplete tasks once you are at home.

- If you work from home, dedicate a corner or room to work-related tasks, and leave that place once your work hours end. For example, if you choose to work in your basement or study room, leave it at 6 PM—if that's when your work hours end—and do not go back there—unless it's necessary—until your work hours start the next day.

- Inform all your team members, colleagues, superiors, and clients of your work hours, and do not attend to their calls, emails, and text messages past your working hours.

- If possible, dedicate a separate phone for work-related tasks and communication, and do not use it once your work hours end.

- When you reach home, make a conscious effort not to discuss work-related problems or talk about work with family and loved ones unless it is necessary. For instance, share news of your promotion with your partner, but don't keep rambling about how a colleague dressed that day.

- When you get home from work, engage in relaxing activities like warm showers or baths, reading books, watching relaxing movies, or just talking with loved ones. Do whatever make you happy and helps you unwind and feel ready to take on your tasks the next day.

If you try these hacks, soon enough, you will feel more involved in your work, and the thought of it will stop feeling draining:

#7: Take breaks

Japanese minimalism is about going slow and enjoying every moment you experience. You cannot do that if you don't infuse breaks into your work routine.

It is good to work consistently but working for several consecutive hours is harmful to your physical and emotional wellbeing.

Your body and mind need rest. If you don't give them this rest, you push yourself way past your limits. Your muscles and body tissues that work throughout the day need to rest to repair. Similarly, your brain—even though it is never really asleep—needs some peace and calm to focus on memory formation instead of actively working on planning and analyzing things.

To energize both your body and brain, take breaks every few hours. You could have a big, one-hour break at mid-day coupled with a small 10 to 15-minute breaks every 2 hours. By infusing breaks into your work routine, you will offer your body and mind sufficient time to rest, recharge, and focus better on work.

#8: Declutter your workspace

Just as you eliminated unnecessary stuff from your house, do the same with your workplace.

Whether you have a small cubicle, a single workspace desk, or an entire office, go through it in detail, pick every item you have, and ask yourself if it sparks joy. Be honest with your feelings and then get rid of unnecessary stationery items, folders, files, furniture, ornaments, storage boxes, cabinet sets, etc. that have stopped serving their purpose and are now lying aimlessly at a corner.

Instead of keeping large piles of documents, create soft copies of all essential documents and save them in a drive on the Cloud. Doing this saves a lot of time, effort, and energy that you would otherwise dedicate to maintaining that data. It also helps you create more space in your office because when you don't have scores of files to maintain and save, you don't need lots of storage cabinets and drawers, making it easier to have a decluttered, tidy office.

#9: Adopt the right mindset

Your life—more so its state—is a reflection of your mood, thoughts, and choices. If you are not enjoying your work, or you find it draining, it's most likely because you don't nurture the right mindset and beliefs about it.

You have to make a conscious effort to love your work, which can only happen when you improve your mindset. Here're approaches you can use to do that:

- When you start your work every day, be grateful for it, and think of how it adds value to your life. Being thankful for your work helps you feel happy about it, thereby allowing you to engage in your tasks with motivation.

- Recall the good days at work, think of why they were good, and engage in those activities to re-live the same experiences. For instance, if one of your memories is of a team lunch, have lunch breaks with your team, share your food, and engage in light-hearted conversations to release your work-related tensions.

- When working on a task, engage your five senses in the experience by focusing on how it feels, anything you can smell, and focus on every detail of the endeavor. Doing this immerses you in the process, helping you enjoy it more.

- Whenever you think of something else or whenever worry pops into your mind as you are working on a task, acknowledge that unnecessary thinking has occurred, and consciously bring your attention back to what you are doing. This strategy takes time and effort to master, but if you consistently work on it, you will develop the habit of being mindful of your work and carrying it out with increased interest.

- Start saying no to any additional projects, tasks, and activities thrown your way. It'll help you avoid overburdening yourself and make sure you only engage in roles that excite you. If your boss assigns you a task that does not fall under your job description, politely say no, and if unethical behavior ensues, report it to the HR department. If you run a business, think of your core values, strengths, and meaningful goals, and use them to ensure that the only projects you undertake are meaningful ones.

As you implement these guidelines gradually, you will notice a remarkable shift in how you feel about your work; you will also get rid of lots of psychological, material, and work-related clutter from your professional life.

#10: Become process-oriented

Remember to become more process-oriented instead of goal-oriented. Yes, you should keep your eyes on the goal, but if you recall the seven principles of Zen and Wabi Sabi, you will realize the essentialness of being present at the moment and enjoying what you are doing.

Enjoying the journey is incredibly important if you're to make the most of what you have and relish every experience. When you focus on the process in the present, you start to live your life, one moment, and one day at a time, which helps you clear chaos, stress, and noise from your mind and spaces.

Having learned how to apply Japanese minimalism to your professional life, take action, and implement the various tips, hacks, and strategies you have learned. Remember, it is good to talk the talk, but you won't yield the desired results if you don't walk the walk.

Starting today, right now even, incorporate these strategies into your work life so that you can make it as meaningful, memorable, and thriving as possible.

In the next chapter, we shall discuss how you can use Japanese Minimalism to build a healthy and meaningful lifestyle that revolves around good health, fitness, and happiness.

7.

HOW TO CREATE A JAPANESE MINIMALISM INSPIRED LIFESTILE

Socrates, one of the most renowned philosophers to date, once beautifully said,

> *"The secret of happiness, you see, is not found in seeking more, but in developing the capacity to enjoy less".*

"Less is more" is the mantra of Japanese minimalism, that, if observed closely, will reveal itself true.

So far, we have learned how to build a Wabi-Sabi mindset that helps you eliminate unnecessary clutter from your house and how to unclutter your professional life. These changes allow you to feel free and internally happy.

Since a lifestyle is more than about your home and work life, it's vital that you also inject Japanese minimalism into other areas of your lifestyle to ensure you live a fulfilling and more meaningful life.

In this chapter, we shall discuss how you can infuse Japanese minimalism into your health, fitness, diet, sleep routine, activities, and social life to create a rich, thriving lifestyle.

Minimalism and Food

Sadly, consumerism has strongly influenced our food choices and eating habits. Today, many of us are often thinking about the next meal while having the current one, a phenomenon that leaves us feeling dissatisfied.

When it comes to food, most of us make unhealthy choices such as opting for junk, processed, and packaged foods that, although tantalizing, hardly benefit us in any way.

Adverts of people enjoying carbonated beverages and bonding over hamburgers leave us feeling that our happiness will come from eating such foods. That's how consumerism and advertisements play with our minds, and unfortunately, we allow them to do so.

For example, if you open your refrigerator, you are likely to find more packaged and processed food items than fresh, whole foods. While packaged and processed food items are more convenient, if eating them becomes a regular part of your life, good health will elude you.

When you do away with unnecessary clutter from your life, you will automatically have less to do. When your in-tray is not full of meaningless tasks, you will have time to devote to cooking meals at home and shall be in a position to opt for seemingly-less convenient, but healthier food choices.

Convenience does not just come from doing things fast; it also comes from slowing down. When you enjoy what you eat, and know it is good for you, you feel at ease, and convenience starts flowing freely in your life.

Additionally, eating healthy and applying minimalism to your food means only eating as much as you need to and when necessary.

Sales, discount options, and deals mess with our mind, causing us to think we need, for example, a carton of juice packs and a big bag of cheese because they are on offer even though you know you won't use them.

If you open your kitchen cabinet or pantry, you are likely to see many food items you haven't touched in ages and many that are rotting away after expiring. The things you bought hoping to save a few bucks often end up wasted, meaning you end up saving nothing after all.

You need to save money; there's no doubt about that. However, if you are only going to waste it, it is useless to buy six packets of biscuits for the price of three if the extra three will end up in the trash can. Think of all those who could benefit from the food that goes to waste every day only because people don't eat what they need and are hungry to consume food rather than enjoy it.

Japanese minimalism frees you from the madness of wanting more and devouring food without enjoying and experiencing it. It focuses on helping you enjoy what you eat and experiencing the magic of every bite, all the while saving food.

Here's how Japanese minimalism makes that possible:

- First, it helps you understand that processed, packaged, junk, and frozen foods harm you because they're rich in trans-fats, genetically modified organisms (GMOs), artificial ingredients, processed sugars and salt, and harmful chemicals. These foods increase your risk of health problems such as diabetes, high blood pressure (hypertension), cardiovascular disorders, neurological problems, obesity, and scores of other health issues.

- Next, minimalism helps you slowly eliminate processed, packaged, and unhealthy food items from your diet. In their place, you consume lean meat cuts, veggies, mostly dark and leafy greens, fresh fruits, nuts, seeds, organic dairy products, whole wheat foods, and home-cooked meals. These foods provide your body with the right amount of proteins, carbohydrates, good fats, fiber, minerals, and the vitamins your body needs for optimal functioning.

- Instantly transforming your diet and replacing unhealthy foods with healthier options can be overwhelming. Minimalism can help you overcome that by adopting a gradual approach to healthy eating. Every week, work on one category of food and cleanse it of unhealthy foods. For instance, if you buy packaged sweet and savory items, use natural foods to prepare snacks and desserts at home. Similarly, if you consume lots of packaged and carbonated beverages, shift to making smoothies, shakes, and juices at home using natural ingredients, spices, and flavoring.

- Japanese minimalism also helps you start paying attention to your food consumption and buy items accordingly every few days, or weekly. Many of us do monthly grocery, which seems like a time-saving and efficient option but is a cause for buying more than we need, thereby wasting money. Buy only a few food items every week and consume them first before buying more. If you use butter, jam, and bread every day for breakfast, but your partner does not eat any of the three, buy a small bar of butter, a jar of jam, and a small loaf of bread that you can consume in a few days.

- Every time you shop for food, go through your refrigerator, pantry, and cabinets to become aware of the items you have so you can purchase suitably.

- When you sit to have a meal, instead of piling heaps of food on your plate, take a small helping first, then after eating it mindfully, if you need more, get another small serving.

- While eating a meal, take a small bite, and chew it properly for about 20 to 30 times. Pay attention to every flavor and texture you experience and enjoy every moment. Take another bite only after finishing the previous one. We often stuff our mouths with food and keep throwing in bite after bite without considering whether we are hungry. We associate unnecessary meaning to eating more and end up being obese and unhappy instead of content and joyous. Slowly, change and slow down your food-eating process. Enjoy every bite, eat slowly, and tune into your tummy before taking a second serving of a meal. If you feel hungry, take another helping. If not, eat later. The more you do this, the easier mindful eating and staying healthy and lean shall become.

- When you sit to have a meal, ensure you're in a calm environment, free from your TV—where possible. Most of us are in the habit of watching something while eating, which seems fine on the surface, but takes our mind off the meal, causing you to eat mindlessly, often more than we need.

- If you do not eat much and weigh less than the healthy average body weight of a person of your age, height, and gender, start eating more. Minimalism in food does not mean eating less; it's more about eating what and when you need to. If you feel weak and lethargic, your body does not have the nutrition it needs to stay healthy. Start adding more nutritious foods to your diet and increase the frequency of your meals. Munch on fruits and nuts, sip smoothies and eat power-packed foods such as quinoa, avocadoes, eggs, and broccoli regularly. Also, monitor your body weight to ensure you don't eat too much or too little than you need.

Keep a food journal and record your daily observations and practices in it. When you introduce avocadoes and Greek yogurt to your diet, write about it in your notebook, with daily updates. This way, you will track how well you have been eating and whether you have been applying Japanese minimalism to your food and eating habits.

Minimalism and Sleep

When you don't sleep well for two nights in a row, you will feel like banging your head against a wall. You become irritable, cranky, and look for people and reasons to blame for your frustration.

When sleepless nights become the norm in your life, it lowers your sense of wellbeing, energy, and productivity. Your body and mind need to relax, and if you don't provide them with ample rest, you will not be able to function optimally or feel good about yourself.

On average, adults need about 7-9 hours of sleep. If you consistently deprive your body of this amount of sleep, you will experience mood swings and a lack of motivation. Japanese minimalism focuses on living a balanced, happy life, which you cannot do if you don't feel at peace, and is where a good night's sleep comes in.

Sleep can improve your mood, confidence, ability to think clearly and focus better, and physical health, more so when you get a good night's sleep regularly.

Here is what you should do to apply minimalism to your sleep routine:

- First, observe the number of hours you sleep every night daily by recording your sleeping and waking hours.

- If you sleep anywhere from 4 to 6 hours, you need to increase the duration of your sleep.

- Since doing this is challenging, adopt a gradual approach by adding 10 to 20 minutes more to your sleep daily until you sleep for 7 to 8 hours every day.

- Set a fixed bedtime, and about an hour before it, stop using any gadgets if possible.

- Engage in something relaxing that soothes your body and mind, and helps you initiate sleep quickly. You can listen to some soothing music or white noises, do some light reading, or take a warm shower; do what works for you.

- Make sure you don't engage in any rigorous activity such as exercise, cycling, or any physical activity that excites your mind and body too close to your bedtime. Schedule such activities to 3 to 4 hours before your bedtime.

- If you have decided to sleep at 11 PM and wake up at 6 AM, go to bed around 10 PM. However, if you are using the slow and steady approach, hit the bed 20 minutes before your usual sleeping time. For example, if you sleep at 2 AM, go to bed around 1:30 AM, and keep going to bed a few minutes earlier every day until you hit your target.

- In the beginning, you are likely to toss and turn in bed; that's normal. When you do, stay put, and even if you feel like using your phone, don't.

Soon enough, your body will adjust to this new routine, and you will start sleeping comfortably.

- Wake up at the set time and tell yourself how good you feel even if you couldn't sleep well at night. The human mind believes whatever you tell it with conviction. If you affirm that you have slept well, it will accept that.

- Moreover, make sure your bedroom has a comfortable environment conducive to sleep. Dim the lights before going to bed to create a soothing environment; check if your mattress, pillows, and bed covers are comfortable and make certain the temperature is neither too hot nor too cold. Comfort is vital to restful sleep.

Start applying these guidelines today, and consistently go to bed earlier and at the same time every day. Developing a good sleep routine will take a while, but with consistency, you can do it—and anything else for that matter.

Once you start sleeping better, you will notice a phenomenal improvement in your mood. You will smile more, think clearly enough to make healthier decisions, and find it easier to reflect on your thoughts, aspirations, and needs.

Minimalism and Fitness

If you are not physically fit, you are not healthy, and an unhealthy body cannot function well at all.

When applied to fitness, Minimalism refers to giving your body the mobility and activity it needs to stay energetic, agile, and functioning optimally.

We often people go overboard with fitness and exercise for hours. On the surface, this seems like a good thing, but in actuality, it results in an over-exhausted body. On the other hand, some of us live exceedingly sedentary lifestyles to the extent that we don't can't get up to fetch a glass of water.

Both spectrums of these lifestyles are extreme, and not even close to what Japanese minimalism professes.

Japanese minimalism is about balance, harmony, and doing things in moderation. To live well, you need to have an active lifestyle, which means you must exercise and stay active in moderation.

Here is what you need to do to attain that:

- Observe your current lifestyle closely. If it only revolves around using automated gadgets, easily accessible options, and delegating tasks, leaving you moving very little, you have a sedentary lifestyle; you need to correct it as soon as possible!

- Start by walking more. That does not mean you should start walking a mile or two daily. You can start running your errands and look for chances to walk more. If you have to reach your office on the third floor, ditch the elevator and use the stairs. If someone is at the door, don't use the intercom, walk up, and personally attend to the door. If you need groceries from a store that's a 5-minute walking distance away, don't ask them to deliver the things at home; stroll there yourself. The more you walk, the more active you become.

- After a few days of walking more, add some exercise or physical activity to your routine. Begin with 5 minutes of aerobics, yoga, Pilates, cycling, or anything else you like. Then, slowly increase the duration to 10 minutes after five days.

- If you can engage in 2 to 3 physical activities of 10 minutes each day, that would be amazing. You could play badminton with friends for 10 minutes, jog for another 10 minutes in the morning, and cycle for 10 minutes late in the evening. Keep increasing the duration of your physical activities until your exercise routine is 50 to 60 minutes long.

- After every 2 to 3 hours of sitting, get up, stretch your legs and arms, and move around. You could do a few jumping jacks or just stretch your body.

In a couple of weeks, you will become more active and able to start enjoying your life more.

Minimalism and Relationships

Your relationships are an integral part of your life. Unfortunately, we tend to take relations for granted or gravitate towards people who are unhealthy for us.

Minimalism in relationships refers to identifying the beautiful and meaningful relationships you wish to maintain and nurture with love, care, and attention.

Here's what you should do:

- First, consider all your current relationships, including with your partner, kids, siblings, parents, friends, etc. and figure out how they influence you.

- To find the weak areas, pay attention to the problems you experience in every relationship.

- Also, identify any relationship that is weighing you down. For instance, if you are having too many marital problems, it is time to discuss them openly.

- Talk to your loved ones about the problems you are experiencing and figure out if they feel the same way.

- If a relationship feels exceptionally toxic, it is best to walk away from it. However, before making that decision, openly discuss the issues with the other person to see if you can come to an agreement. If it does not work out, stop interacting with the person, and taking or responding to their calls.

- As you break free from the toxic people in your life, you will create more room and time for authentic relations.

- Start paying more attention to the needs of your loved ones, reach out to them, and make sure you spend quality time with them regularly. You don't need to spend hours of your day with your kids. Just focus on spending quality time together over a meal, a movie, some music, or a conversation. When spending time with loved ones, put your phone and other gadgets away and give them your undivided attention.

- Also, express your love and feelings to them by saying out loud, exchanging practical gifts—avoid unnecessary gifts— and through sweet gestures. You could cook meals for your loved ones, help them solve problems, or do things that please them.

- Likewise, observe your social life and activities, and gradually reduce the time you spend on contacts and activities that don't bring you joy. If you only spend time with your boss to get a promotion out of it, stop doing that. Spend the same time with your best friend; even though a raise won't come from it, you'll smile more and be happier.

As you distance yourself from the toxic people in your life and surround yourself with those who love you genuinely, you will become more and more peaceful and happier.

Minimalism and Finances

Consumerism is the primary cause of overspending. Think about it:

When you see something that catches your fancy, you drool over it, and the next minute, you are emptying your wallet to purchase it. That is not how things should be, especially for an authentic Japanese minimalist.

Just as you decluttered your life and freed it from unhealthy relations, eating habits, and unnecessary stuff, commit to getting rid of unnecessary expenses and streamlining your finances.

Here's how to do that:

- Assess your net income and expenditure.

- Of those expenses, define the bare necessities and set a budget for them.

- Determine which purchases and expenses consume too much of your money without any benefit to match. For instance, if you don't watch cable TV, but pay $500 for it, get rid of it. Similarly, if you have a gym membership, but hardly visit it, cancel it.

- Make a conscious effort to save about $10 to $100 every week and set it aside.

- Slowly grow your funds; keep some as petty cash and invest the rest in a good policy—insurance, health, etc.—, funds, or business that gives you a good return.

- At the same time, consciously say no to yourself every time you feel the need to make a big purchase. After doing that a few times, you'll become more conscious or your spending patterns, making it easier to say no to yourself when you're about to make unnecessary purchases.

Once you get in the habit of spending money wisely and only when needed, your bank balance will start growing, and your need to work around the clock will dissipate.

Minimalism and Spirituality

Spirituality is a subjective term whose meaning varies from person to person.

That notwithstanding, a common consensus is that spirituality is about knowing your purpose and direction in life.

As you slow down and eliminate meaningless activities from your life, you create space to reflect more on what you want, a process that helps you get in tune with your purpose, thereby making you more spiritual.

Here's what you need to do:

- Dedicate 10 minutes of your day to meditating on your thoughts, dreams, aspirations, etc.

- Start by breathing in your natural manner and watching your breath as you inhale and exhale.

- Try to become one with your breath, which you can do by observing it mindfully.

- Every time you drift off in thought, bring your attention back to your breath.

- After a few sessions, you'll get the hang of it and become more conscious of your breath.

- When that happens, and as you get better at the practice, it'll become easier to pick one thought and reflect on it.

- When you get to that point, start asking yourself questions about what you want to do in life, where you want to head, and your purpose in this life.

- Write down the answers you get and consider them as often as possible until you distill invaluable insight.

- After a while, you'll be able to establish a nexus between your findings and figure out what you want, including how minimalism can help you do that.

Once you start working on all these areas, little by little, your life will start becoming more tranquil, peaceful, and happier.

CONCLUSIONS

I trust that you found this book helpful and that what you've learned helps you gain freedom from consumerism, media biases, and societal expectations.

As we part ways, remember that Japanese minimalism can help you unlock your best life ever. All you have to do is start taking action to implement it in different areas of your life.

If you enjoyed this book, please let me know your thoughts by leaving a short review on amazon. Thank you!

BIBLIOGRAPHY

https://amzn.to/3hPyH7u

https://www.lifehack.org/595106/why-being-a-minimalist-at-work-can-make-you-more-successful

https://medium.com/@WeAreMobile1st/how-minimalism-can-help-you-achieve-the-perfect-work-life-balance-98fe54654499

http://www.jacmcneil.com/2018/02/01/5-ways-to-bring-minimalism-to-your-work/

https://www.theminimalists.com/

https://medium.com/personal-growth/wabi-sabi-the-japanese-philosophy-for-a-perfectly-imperfect-life-11563e833dc0

https://miraimist.com/2017/09/11/wabi-sabi-ism-the-essence-of-minimalism/

https://blog.society6.com/how-the-ancient-art-of-wabi-sabi-can-modernize-your-space/#:~:text=Derived%20from%20Buddhist%20teachings%2C%20Wabi,design%20aesthetic%20into%20your%20life.

https://www.hotelzen.jp/blog/japanese-minimalism-wabi-sabi-ma/

https://vancouversun.com/life/fashion-beauty/the-great-debate-the-difference-between-japanese-and-scandinavian-minimalist-style

https://medium.com/@slowwco/konmari-method-5-step-decluttering-cheat-sheet-a1d1cc873e17#:~:text=The%20KonMari%20Method%20in%205%20Steps&text=Categories%20(in%20order)%3A%20Clothes,)%2C%20and%20lastly%2C%20mementos.

https://www.thestatesman.com/opinion/in-japan-less-is-more-1502505355.html

https://www.lionsroar.com/what-is-zen-buddhism-and-how-do-you-practice-it/

https://greentumble.com/the-negative-effects-of-consumerism/#:~:text=As%20well%20as%20obvious%20social,accelerated%20climate%20change%20%5B4%5D.

https://www.washingtonpost.com/national/health-science/hoarding-is-serious-disorder--and-its-only-getting-worse-in-the-us/2016/04/11/b64a0790-f689-11e5-9804-537defcc3cf6_story.html

JAPANESE MINIMALISM

https://www.lifehack.org/articles/lifestyle/top-8-benefits-living-minimalist-lifestyle.html

https://brightside.me/creativity-home/4-apartments-of-japanese-minimalists-that-can-make-you-realize-how-much-junk-there-is-in-your-life-704560/

https://japanahome.com/journal/japanese-minimalism-japan-can-teach-living-simply/

https://medium.com/the-minimalist/how-to-strengthen-your-minimalist-practice-with-wabi-sabi-79e2015f16eb

https://www.hunker.com/13709932/11-ways-to-do-japanese-minimalism-right

https://www.sapporo.co.uk/news/the-art-of-less-is-more-japanese-minimalism-and-its-influence-on-western-design-aesthetics/

https://www.japantimes.co.jp/life/2017/08/13/lifestyle/taking-minimalism-next-level/

https://www.businessinsider.com/inside-japans-extremely-minimalist-homes-2016-6#part-of-the-minimalist-philosophy-is-keeping-together-the-objects-that-belong-together-20

https://www.independent.co.uk/life-style/christmas/travel/32-photos-show-how-obsessed-japan-minimalism-a8023296.html

https://yunomi.life/blogs/discover/declutter-your-mind-with-japanese-minimalism

https://www.sapporo.co.uk/news/the-art-of-less-is-more-japanese-minimalism-and-its-influence-on-western-design-aesthetics/#:~:text=Inspired%20by%20the%20spartan%20aesthetic,ancient%20customs%20and%20a%20love

https://www.insider.com/inside-japans-extremely-minimalist-homes-2016-6

https://www.treehugger.com/cultural-concept-ma-heart-japanese-minimalism-4858440

https://www.tokyoweekender.com/2019/02/how-japan-made-me-a-minimalist/

https://www.apa.org/monitor/jun04/maxed

https://www.apa.org/monitor/2008/07-08/consumerism